Critical Essays on the Writings of Lillian Smith

vi   Contents

127 **CHAPTER 6**
Positive Self-Identity: Neighborliness in Lillian Smith's *Memory of a Large Christmas*
—*April Conley Kilinski*

149 **CHAPTER 7**
Hatred and Hope in the American South: Rhetorical Excavations in Lillian Smith's *Our Faces, Our Words*
—*David Brauer*

173 Contributors

175 Index

Contents

3   Spinning Bridges: An Introduction
     —*Tanya Long Bennett*

21   **CHAPTER 1**
     Mind Where You Puts Yo Feet: A Study of Southern Boundaries
       in Lillian Smith's *Strange Fruit*
     —*Tanya Long Bennett*

41   **CHAPTER 2**
     Ghosts of Our Fathers: Rewriting the South in Lillian Smith's *Killers
       of the Dream*
     —*Justin Mellette*

57   **CHAPTER 3**
     "The Intricate Weavings of Unnumbered Threads": Personal and
       Societal Trauma in Lillian Smith's *Killers of the Dream*
     —*Emily Pierce Cummins*

87   **CHAPTER 4**
     Martha, Mary, and Susie: Totalitarian Political Ideology and
       Women in Lillian Smith's *The Journey*
     —*Wendy Kurant Rollins*

109   **CHAPTER 5**
     Reading *One Hour* in the Time of #MeToo
     —*Cameron Williams Crawford*

The University Press of Mississippi is the scholarly publishing agency of the Mississippi Institutions of Higher Learning: Alcorn State University, Delta State University, Jackson State University, Mississippi State University, Mississippi University for Women, Mississippi Valley State University, University of Mississippi, and University of Southern Mississippi.

www.upress.state.ms.us

The University Press of Mississippi is a member of the Association of University Presses.

Any discriminatory or derogatory language or hate speech regarding race, ethnicity, religion, sex, gender, class, national origin, age, or disability that have been retained or appear in elided form is in no way an endorsement of the use of such language outside a scholarly context.

Copyright © 2021 by University Press of Mississippi
All rights reserved
Manufactured in the United States of America

First printing 2021
∞

Library of Congress Cataloging-in-Publication Data

Names: Bennett, Tanya Long, editor.
Title: Critical essays on the writings of Lillian Smith / edited by Tanya Long Bennett.
Description: Jackson : University Press of Mississippi, 2021. | Includes bibliographical references and index.
Identifiers: LCCN 2021031176 (print) | LCCN 2021031177 (ebook) | ISBN 9781496836847 (hardback) | ISBN 9781496836854 (trade paperback) | ISBN 9781496836861 (epub) | ISBN 9781496836878 (epub) | ISBN 9781496836885 (pdf) | ISBN 9781496836892 (pdf)
Subjects: LCSH: Smith, Lillian (Lillian Eugenia), 1897–1966—Criticism and interpretation. | American literature—Southern States—History and criticism. | American literature—Women authors—History and criticism.
Classification: LCC PS3537.M653 Z63 2021 (print) | LCC PS3537.M653 (ebook) | DDC 813/.52—dc23
LC record available at https://lccn.loc.gov/2021031176
LC ebook record available at https://lccn.loc.gov/2021031177

British Library Cataloging-in-Publication Data available

Critical Essays on the Writings of

LILLIAN SMITH

Edited by Tanya Long Bennett

University Press of Mississippi / Jackson

Critical Essays on the Writings of Lillian Smith

Spinning Bridges: An Introduction

—Tanya Long Bennett

> Making up stories is both reaching back into memory for things we've stored there and reaching forward into the world we've heard about. It takes imagination to do both. I like to think of it also as spinning a bridge which connects my world with your world, and with other people's worlds. (Lillian Smith, "Children Talking" 135)

Lillian Eugenia Smith understood that when we open a book, we seek adventure. As long as the odds of survival seem reasonably high, we readily abandon the familiar for the unknown, leaving the oft-trodden path in hopes of strange landscapes. Because we have played so often in the security of our own "home" garden—the carefully cultivated place of our imagination where we navigate with confidence the daily challenges of living—we come to a new book as if peeking through the gate, yearning for fresh territories to explore. Although our gardens are ostensibly safe from dangers like hungry panthers, taboo sexual behaviors, and unpredictably malevolent divinities, the garden walls are tall and made of solid stone, obscuring the views beyond and hence new insights into ourselves and the universe. Curious beings that we are, even among the fragrant flowers that grow here, we often feel stifled by the enclosure that we have helped to build and maintain. When we open a book's cover, we are in the mood to follow the author somewhere *beyond* these walls, even into panther territory if necessary, but under one important condition: that the world portrayed is imbued, even if only subtly, with *optimism*.

The artist faces a mighty challenge in designing such a journey. If, to minimize readers' anxieties and lure them out through the garden gate, she paints the frontier with too much sentimentality, the project's power will be undermined, offering only the *pretense* of new territory, and thus no real self-discovery. Any good reader will realize the trick and demand his money back. Conversely, a book that eschews *all* the motives associated with garden tending renders futile the very act of writing itself. If we fear that we are being led out of the walls simply for the purpose of being fed to the panther, most of us will reverse our course the moment we are able and "escape" back into the garden, slamming the gate shut behind us. Even boredom is, for most readers, preferable to a perspective that does not allow for goodness, connection, or growth.

Smith was well aware of this challenge, since she wrote, at least in part, to southern readers about the South. Smith herself believed in the possibility of a better world that could be realized only by leaving the garden, and she wrote to draw readers toward this vision. In *Now Is the Time*, for example, she addresses the fears of her white neighbors after the *Brown v. Board of Education* decision of 1954: "There is a feeling which most [whites] share: anxiety. They do not know how integration will work out. They are, suddenly, fearing the old threat they heard in childhood. 'Bad things will happen,' they were told ten thousand times. What bad things? No one quite knows" (78). To lead reticent readers out of the garden and into uncharted territory, she offers through her words a bridge of understanding and hope: "There are things we can say and things we can do. . . . They count in building a mood of good will in your community; they reduce tension in your own mind; they encourage others to act creatively" (81–82). Her sympathies lay not only with her nervous fellow whites. To the contrary, she worked tirelessly, if not always successfully, to imagine what midcentury America must be like for marginalized residents of all ilks: "What role do esteem and acceptance play in a child's life? How do his feelings affect his capacity to learn, his values, his image of himself?" (*Now Is the Time* 80). Smith's writings evince

Spinning Bridges: An Introduction

a deep sympathy for a vast range of readers, which serves her well in spinning bridges from one imagination to another.[1] For writers like Smith, a lost chance to experience wild and fertile landscapes is equivalent to a kind of death. She was convinced that we can thrive together only with the gate open, with bridges connecting each garden to other landscapes, one imagination to another.

Smith's perspective on the artist's role has fascinated readers since she began publishing in the late 1930s, and her notion of the writer's relationship to her or his fellows is profoundly relevant to us in 2021. Consider the following passage from her 1960 essay "Novelists Need a Commitment":

> We can never face and master our ordeal by working on it one level at a time. We can do it only by an in-depth simultaneity of effort: of individual, group, nation. On every known level of experience[,] artist, scientist, preacher, politician, teacher, laborer, and industrialist, young and old, must pool their talents and skills, their imagination and knowledge, their symbols and their technologies, their metaphors and their dreams, their hope and their compassion. All this for what? To create a new kind of person, a new kind of life on this earth. (18)

Smith wrote this passage in the face of Cold War nuclear threat and roiling southern racial relations, but her words might just as aptly have addressed a twenty-first-century world plagued by climate change, global power mongering, and ideological division, in spite of the internet's incredible potential to connect people across borders, physical and otherwise. The bridges Smith spun with her writings—fiction as well as nonfiction—apply powerfully to the issues we grapple with today. As an activist, she made an impact, as many have recognized, but her optimism about improving society was inextricably tied to her artistic impulse. When the Women's Division of the American Jewish Congress awarded her the first Queen Esther Scroll, Smith urged in her acceptance speech the necessity of the poetic in times of social crisis:

Once we see it: once we begin to realize, by act of imagination and heart, the meaning of what is happening to us, once we feel the direction we are going, then things will fall in line, chaos will resolve into new forms. And it is the poet's job to show us. For only the poet can look beyond details at the total picture; only the poet can feel the courage beyond fear, only he can grasp the splinters and bend them into a new wholeness that does not yet exist. ("The Role of the Poet in a World of Demagogues" 161–62)

Extending well beyond the political, her strong belief in the necessity of linking our imaginations to transform the world shaped her writing and ensured its resonance over time.

Smith's Development as a Writer

Smith's first published book, *Strange Fruit*, generated great public acclaim with its appearance in 1944. Tracing the tragic love affair of a black woman and white man, each trying to navigate the mores of a small southern town, the novel quickly became a best seller, and its censorship by the US Postal Service only increased the book's capital as a literary tour de force (Loveland 71). By the time of this debut novel's publication, however, Smith had been writing for years, and *Strange Fruit*'s aesthetic sophistication and sociological insight were a result of the author's complex formative experiences.

Born in 1897 in Jasper, Florida, to a relatively privileged family, Smith was the seventh child of nine. In *Memory of a Large Christmas*, she describes scenes from her childhood, characterizing her own child persona as "little miss Curious," who early on observes and processes the world around her in distinctly writerly ways. When Smith was a teen, the family business failed, and the Smiths moved to their Clayton, Georgia, summer home, where her father opened and operated the Laurel Falls Camp for Girls. After high school, Smith attended Piedmont College, in Demorest, Georgia, for a year before

Spinning Bridges: An Introduction

heading to Peabody Conservatory to study piano. Soon abandoning her aspirations of becoming a career musician, however, she traveled to Huzhou, China (now Wuxing, Zhejiang), in 1922, to serve as head of the music department for the Methodist Virginia School (Blackwell and Clay 11). Here she was exposed to Chinese culture and people, observing great wealth as well as great poverty and gaining insights into human behavior and world politics, particularly the ways that European colonialism had affected China and India.[2]

In 1925, when word came that her father's health was declining, she returned to the United States and took over administration of the Laurel Falls Camp. Despite the demands of her new position, she regularly wrote and distributed a small camp newsletter, the *Laurel Leaf*. Further, in 1930, she started a novel about six young white women from the US South who teach at a missionary school in China. Titles tentatively assigned to the novel draft included "Walls" and "And the Waters Flow On." Between 1930 and 1935, she also drafted a novel titled "Tom Harris and Family," set in a small southern town and tracing the story of a family much like her own. During this period, she wrote three novellas, as well. None of these novel manuscripts was ever published, and all five were destroyed in a 1955 fire at Smith's Laurel Falls home (Loveland 17). Yet this artistic and intellectual incubation period surely fostered Smith's maturation and helped refine her literary skills.

Undoubtedly, she benefited during this time from her budding relationship with Paula Snelling, a math teacher who worked as counselor at Laurel Falls Camp. Similarly bright and energetic, the two developed strong intellectual and creative bonds, ultimately becoming life partners, though they were not public about their intimacy. Snelling proved an adept reader for Smith's writings, even cofounding with her in 1936 a "little magazine" called *Pseudopodia*, which they renamed the *North Georgia Review* in 1937 and *South Today* in 1942. By 1944, Smith had written and published many essays and columns, and her work, travel, reading, and writing experiences had contributed to her growth as an artist; *Strange Fruit* evidences not only her ability to translate personal experience into compelling narrative but also great proficiency at editing and polishing a manuscript for public release (Loveland 18). Although she would not publish another best seller in her lifetime, by the mid-1940s, she had "come into her own" as an intellectual and a writer.

Over the next two decades, Smith went on to publish the autobiographical *Killers of the Dream* (1949); her socioaesthetic "confession" *The Journey* (1954); *Now Is the Time* (1955), a brief but incisive instruction manual for building on the *Brown v. Board of Education* decision; *One Hour* (1959), a novel exploring the potential damage of McCarthyist paranoia; the autobiographical *Memory of a Large Christmas* (1962); and *Our Faces, Our Words* (1964), a genre-defying collage of fictionalized first-person commentaries and images, reflecting the perspectives of characters, both black and white, on events of the civil rights era. From 1944 to 1966, when Smith succumbed to cancer, her fame grew as she continued to release books, offer public speeches, and publish essays in periodicals such as *Redbook, Life, Saturday Review, The Progressive, New Republic,* and *New York Times Magazine* (Blackwell and Clay 12–14).

Yet Smith's reputation during her lifetime and for many years afterward was based primarily on her activism rather than her literary accomplishment. She complained about this predicament, alleging that "even the most generous of the white critics had failed to treat the novel [*Strange Fruit*] as literature" (Loveland 75). In a 1965 letter to Wilma Dykeman Stokely, Smith expressed her chagrin at being cast so reductively: "Am I really going down in history as just the 'brave little woman who spent her life helping Negros' or am I ever going to be acknowledged as the writer I think I am and many Europeans think I am[?]" (333–34). Her legacy played out as she feared it would, at least for a time: as well-known as Smith is today for her role in promoting human rights, her work is conspicuously absent from major literary anthologies, and her writings are rarely taught in college literature courses. As the critical essays in this collection attest, however, to benefit fully from the contributions of this talented writer, we must take into account her literary perspective and practice.

Scholarship on Smith's Writings

Since the mid-1990s, literary study of Lillian Smith has expanded from a minimally tended trail to a narrow but smoothly paved scenic road. The goal of this essay collection is to widen that road and enhance it with improved signage, encouraging further scholarship on this remarkable Georgia author, who lived her belief that as we venture beyond our gardens and cross bridges into unfamiliar territory, "vision will come to us . . . ; imaginations will be stirred. Our ordeal will be transformed into a great creative adventure" (*Now Is the Time* 74).

In 1971, blazing the trail for other scholars, Louise Blackwell and Frances Clay published *Lillian Smith*, a volume in the Twayne United States Authors series, which remains to date the only monograph on the body of Smith's work. In this early study, Blackwell and Clay provide analysis of Smith's fiction and nonfiction, placing her novels in the tradition of naturalism and making the case that they achieve unity "through structure and characterization" (55). Recognizing the influence of Freud on her perspective, these scholars assert that "the behavior of [Smith's] characters is determined by deep psychological frustrations which result in such emotions as anxiety, fear, guilt, hate, love, persecution, and sexual obsession. This behavior, in turn, gives rise to complicated social problems" (65). While this monograph's formalist approach is now somewhat dated, Blackwell and Clay's study established a foundation for the literary studies that followed, pointing scholars toward Smith's strategy of "interweaving past actions and thoughts with present situations to create an awareness of cause and effect" and her achievement of an "economy of language" that "covers a large subject" in distilled and symbolic prose (44).

A year after the publication of the Twayne volume, *From the Mountain* appeared, featuring selected writings by Smith from *South Today*. Edited by Helen White and Redding S. Sugg, the collection evidences Smith's range as a writer. Further expanding access to her work, in 1978, Norton published *The Winner Names the Age: A Collection of Writings*, making available some of Smith's previously unpublished speeches and essays. Michelle Cliff edited the collection, and Paula Snelling wrote the book's preface, asserting Smith's profound effect on the South and society at large through her writing:

> Though they lived in communities indifferent or hostile to [Smith's] ideas, the smaller groups who were her audiences were hungering to hear such words said aloud. Had they not been spoken by someone, in such a manner as she said them, and at such times and places as they were said, the acceleration of change that has occurred in the last quarter-century could not have taken place. (15)

Also appearing during the 1970s and 1980s were a number of articles that helped generate and sustain a steady pace for Smith studies, including Jo Ann Robinson's "Lillian Smith: Reflections on Race and Sex" (1977), Pat B. Brewer's "Lillian Smith: A Thorn in the Flesh of Crackerdom" (1980), and Don Belton's "Lillian Smith: Walking a Trembling Earth" (1983). During this period, scholars included discussion of Smith's work in broad perspectives on southern letters and culture as well, for example, in Morton Sosna's *In Search of the Silent South* (1977), Daniel Joseph Singal's *The War Within: From Victorian to Modernist Thought in the South, 1919–1945* (1982), and Fred Hobson's *Tell about the South: The Southern Rage to Explain* (1983). In the latter, Hobson acknowledges *The Journey* as something like "spiritual autobiography" and describes it as a "Whitmanesque performance, with a persona who dared to take the broken and dispossessed into herself, a compassionate ego expanding to embrace the suffering" (320). Although he seems to agree with figures like Ralph McGill, who complained that Smith could be "a bit dogmatic or firmly naive" (McGill qtd. in Hobson 317), Hobson's treatment of *The Journey* praises the book's poetic effect, arguing that its persona adeptly engages in the liberating process of articulation—of writing and reading in particular.

Producing perhaps the most insightful book-length study of Smith to date, Anne C. Loveland published a 1986 biography titled *Lillian*

Smith: A Southerner Confronting the South. In her prologue, Loveland bemoans scholars'"tendency so far . . . to focus on [Smith's] work in the civil rights movement and to neglect her literary effort" (2). Loveland proceeds to address this gap significantly with her own illuminating examinations of Smith's writings as she traces the author's life. The biographer describes, for example, the impact of *One Hour*'s point of view, that of the rector Dave Landrum. Loveland acknowledges the complaints of Leslie Fiedler that Smith had, in this second novel, "stripped the Modernist point of view of its antisocial, subversive tendencies, and made it into a 'code of genteel sentimentality'" (166), and explains that Fiedler, as well as Smith's friend Lawrence Kubie, a psychoanalyst, objected to the novel's juxtaposition of a deterministic narrative view with Dave's enduring faith in God. Yet Loveland goes on to provide, if not a defense, a clarification of *One Hour*'s alleged internal contradiction. She notes that Smith disliked Sartre's brand of existentialism, which took nihilism as its logical partner. Loveland holds that in her serious consideration of existential philosophy, Smith rejected nihilism. She quotes Smith regarding critics' condemnation of her perspective, which she believed was out of fear: "For if they once accept hope . . . they must accept their responsibility as human beings to do something about the human condition. As long as they can think of the human condition as totally evil, totally absurd, totally unreasonable, totally without sense and totally unchangeable, then why not lie down and suck the nipple of self-pity?" (Smith qtd. in Loveland 167–68). Loveland asserts that "in *One Hour* [Smith] attempted to dramatize the more hopeful brand of existentialism by showing man's capacity for courage, compassion, and transcendence." By the same token, she argues, the novel was an effort to combat the threat posed by nihilism (168). Itself a rich exploration of mid-twentieth-century ideas and politics, Loveland's biography provides a nuanced perspective on the factors that shaped Smith's writings and her literary legacy.

By the mid-1990s, scholarship on Smith's writings was gaining momentum, perhaps as an effect of post-postmodern critique, voicing skepticism that literature could "decenter" without abdicating ethical responsibility altogether. Fueling this acceleration of work on Smith were the research of Margaret Rose Gladney and the establishment of the Lillian E. Smith Center. In 1993, Gladney edited *How Am I to Be Heard? Letters of Lillian Smith*, the result of painstaking and methodical archival work, interviews, and curation. The scope of Gladney's research on Smith extends beyond that of any other scholar heretofore, save perhaps Loveland, springing from a comprehensive examination of Smith's life and writings. In her preface, Gladney explains her fascination with the author and her work:

> My interest in Smith's letters grew out of an oral history project, begun in 1978, in which I interviewed over fifty women throughout the South, including Paula Snelling and various members of Smith's family, who had been campers or counselors at Laurel Falls Camp. I was interested in Smith's work as a southern woman with other southern women, and I soon realized that the camp also played a central role in her development as a writer. While working in the Smith papers at the University of Florida and the University of Georgia, I found the quality and quantity of her correspondence most impressive. Having published three articles on her work with the camp and her portrayal of southern women, I saw in the collected letters a form of self-portrait of the author that vividly displays the variety and interrelatedness of her interests and talents, as well as her fundamental struggle as a woman writer. (xvii)

Adding momentum to Gladney's research, the Lillian E. Smith Center was founded in 2000 on the historic Laurel Springs property, site of the girls' camp that Smith had directed from 1925 to 1948. In 2013, Piedmont College acquired the property, enabling its improved curation and preservation. Listed as a site on the Southern Literary Trail, the center houses a substantial collection of Smith's papers.[3] The LES Center board of trustees, along with Craig Amason, director of the center from 2013 to 2018, and its current director, Matthew Teutsch, have promoted research on Smith's work by publicizing the Laurel Falls site, establishing the Lillian E. Smith Scholars Program, and managing the Smith archives held at Piedmont College.

A member of the LES Center board herself, Gladney went on to collaborate with Lisa Hodgens, a professor of English at Piedmont College, to publish *A Lillian Smith Reader* in 2016, a collection of Smith's writings, many of which had previously been accessible only through archival research. The book's purpose was to "[open] up new possibilities for students of all ages to dip into the vast pool of human wisdom from which Lillian Smith drew and to which she contributed" (Gladney and Hodgens, "Introduction" 3). The volume gathers a wide variety of Smith's publications, including columns, book reviews, and essays from *Pseudopodia*, as well as pieces appearing in *Educational Leadership*, *Georgia Review*, the *Chicago Defender*, the *Atlanta Constitution*, and other periodicals, and excerpts from her books and letters. Providing a systematic perspective of Smith's life and work, the book offers an invaluable tool for Smith scholars. While their introduction and afterword emphasize Smith's commitment to social justice, Gladney and Hodgens's selection of pieces for inclusion in the reader conveys the author's essentially writerly identity: "She told us her stories of travels not only around the world but also deep into her psyche, those inner places most of us dare not go" (302).[4]

Since Gladney's publication of Smith's letters in 1993, dozens more studies have appeared investigating Smith's literary impact, a shift marked not only by an increased volume of research on the author but also by a richer diversity of approaches to her work. Scholars continue to explore her treatment of racial discrimination and its effects, but each new analysis further reveals also her aesthetic agility and literary sensibility. For example, in a 2001 study of *Strange Fruit* and *Killers of the Dream*, McKay Jenkins illuminates Smith's portrayal of the psyche crippled by racism and the mental gymnastics it requires to continue functioning: "Her writing brims with descriptions of children who are spiritually damaged before they can even define what race is and with white women who have become utterly detached from their own physical and spiritual presences" (113). Examining Smith's transcendence of arbitrary race and difference concepts and placing her in context of other well-respected writers, Jay Garcia's 2008 article "Race, Empire, and Humanism in the Work of Lillian Smith" explores the cross-cultural notion of humanism employed in *Killers of the Dream*, a notion that, according to Garcia, was heavily influenced by Smith's reading of Rabindranath Tagore and Mahatma Gandhi. Remarking on Smith's interest in a humanism relevant to postcolonial societies, Garcia asserts, "*Killers of the Dream* can be profitably read as a set of transcultural reflections that undermine the tendency toward unitary forms of identification. Smith implies that the category of southerner no longer carries self-evident meaning, for in investigating Southern culture in terms of internal differentiation and psychological fissures, the stability of the category has diminished" (77). Also recognizing in Smith's writings a flexible, and thus enduring, treatment of humanism, Thomas F. Haddox's 2012 "Lillian Smith, Cold War Intellectual" defends Smith's work against allegations of naive liberal humanism, viewing her, on the contrary, "as a surprisingly representative 'Cold War' intellectual, pressing the claims of individual persons against both political totalitarianism and the degradations of mass culture, and championing a modernist aesthetic as a badge of human autonomy" (53). Focusing his analysis on Smith's less often examined books *The Journey* and *One Hour*, Haddox argues that "for Smith . . . a modernist aesthetic . . . achieves political resonance through its very rejection of overt political content—and thus blurs the line between the aesthetic and the ethical" (53). Although Haddox's study acknowledges Smith's value as a sociopolitical thinker, it emphasizes her literary talents in rendering narratives of significant aesthetic value.

Since the 1990s, several books forwarding updated theories of southern literature—as indicator of and influence on culture and letters—have considered Smith as a key figure in the landscape of southern literature (often insisting that the term "southern" attributes a false notion of homogeneity to the region). Will Brantley's 1993 *Feminine Sense in Southern Memoir: Smith, Glasgow, Welty, Hellman,*

Porter, and Hurston, for example, "situate[s] these authors within a context of Southern feminism and the more inclusive discourse of American liberalism" (x). Further exploring the complex relationship between southern women writers and their environment, in her now-seminal *Dirt and Desire: Reconstructing Southern Women's Writing, 1930–1990* (2000), Patricia Yaeger digs beneath "older models of southern writing" (xv) to examine the aggressively drawn grotesque and outcast, considering the work of Smith alongside that of Zora Neale Hurston, Carson McCullers, Katherine Anne Porter, Sarah E. Wright, and many others. Expanding the study of southern writers beyond a binary gender perspective, Gary Richards includes discussion of Smith's work in his compelling argument for a more complex lens on southern literature in *Lovers and Beloveds: Sexual Otherness in Southern Fiction, 1936–1961* (2005). And further enriching the intersectional view of the southern legacy, in *Entitled to the Pedestal: Place, Race, and Progress in White Southern Women's Writing, 1920–1945* (2011), Nghana Tamu Lewis deconstructs plantation mythology and the myth of white southern womanhood to reveal that their power has lived well beyond the Jim Crow era, despite ostensible intentions of white southern women writers like Smith to subvert plantation mythology. Examination of Smith's work from these southern studies perspectives, whether as positive or negative example, clarifies that she has indeed significantly influenced southern and US letters.

That her writings do not fit neatly into a specific literary movement has spurred scholars to explore more broadly her work's relationship to that of her American contemporaries in efforts to "place" Smith philosophically and aesthetically. The studies that follow this trend illustrate the continued necessity of accounting for Smith's writings in establishing the evolution of American literature at large. In "Richard Weaver, Lillian Smith, the South, and the World" (2016), Robert Brinkmeyer Jr. observes that Smith differed from fellow modernists in her clear ethical stances. He echoes Loveland's comments that while Smith's portrayals of human behavior were shaped heavily by Freud and other structuralists, she was not of the Lost Generation, in that she would not abandon the liberal program and its optimism. Brinkmeyer expands on this comparative context, asserting that neither could she embrace the "Agrarian ideal of the individual in contact with the rhythms of nature" (272), its commitment to "the possibility of romance" (275), and its insistence that social "hierarchies [were] necessary for civilized life" (274). Brinkmeyer explains that "for Smith, defenders of the traditional order, like Weaver and the Agrarians, promulgated an idealized image of the South in which the region's benighted reality—its violent racism, its grinding poverty, its corrupt antidemocratic politics, its blind (and blinding) worship of the past—was entirely absent" (285). In such contexts, Jenkins, Garcia, Haddox, Brinkmeyer, and other twenty-first-century scholars of Smith's work have articulated effectively her continued relevance to literary studies. Moving beyond the New Critics' restrictive mandate of objectivity and the cynicism of (some brands of) postmodernism regarding personal responsibility, scholars are coming to Smith's writings with renewed fervor. Her work has so far held up admirably to investigation from a wide range of approaches, offering valuable insight not only on the mid-twentieth-century American South but also into the creative process and its crucial role in human flourishing.

Overview of the Collection

The essays gathered in this collection build insightfully and provocatively on the foundation of Smith studies, expanding, in particular, the scholarship on Smith's literary prowess and its impact. Reflecting the chronology of Smith's publications, the book is organized to guide readers through the powerful aesthetic and thematic workings of her texts. As readers move through the chapters, they will discover a rich variety of approaches to Smith's writings. In chapter 1, "Mind Where You Puts Yo Feet: A Study of Southern Boundaries in Lillian Smith's *Strange Fruit*," for example, I examine the best-selling novel through a lens of border and whiteness theory. The essay explores geographical markers of the fictional Maxwell, Georgia, to reveal their impact on both the physical movements of the novel's characters and their psychological navigation of a "home" strictly dictating their behaviors. In chapter 2, "Ghosts of Our Fathers: Rewriting the South in Lillian Smith's *Killers of the Dream*," Justin Mellette investigates Smith's portrayal of the South as "hellscape" in the memoir, considering especially her focus on "ghost stories" and other vehicles of racial and paternalistic control that enable the perpetuation of southern violence and terrorism. In chapter 3, "'The Intricate Weavings of Unnumbered Threads': Personal and Societal Trauma in Lillian Smith's *Killers of the Dream*," Emily Pierce Cummins employs trauma theory as a framework for understanding the content, form, and effects of *Killers of the Dream*, elaborating on the literary strategies at work in the autobiographical tome. Cummins argues that the text itself (its writing as well as its reading) serves as a mechanism for processing southern social trauma, both personal and communal.

With chapter 4, "Martha, Mary, and Susie: Totalitarian Political Ideology and Women in Lillian Smith's *The Journey*," the collection shifts toward Smith's later, Cold War–era work. Here Wendy Kurant Rollins provides a close reading of *The Journey*, contending that through adept development of Susie, the motor court owner's wife, Smith illustrates how authoritarian systems cripple female artists, "redirecting them into destructive and self-destructive outlets." Further considering Smith's 1950s writings, in chapter 5, "Reading *One Hour* in the Time of #MeToo," Cameron Williams Crawford looks closely at the stories of the second novel's characters, arguing that Smith's investigation of culture through a first-person narrator generates a provocative tension between critique of "mob mentality" and that of southern misogyny. Crawford holds that in the #MeToo era, this novel has the power to disrupt deep-rooted systems perpetuating sexual violence.

While the literary merits of Smith's *Memory of a Large Christmas* have largely been overlooked, in chapter 6, "Positive Self-Identity: Neighborliness in Lillian Smith's *Memory of a Large Christmas*," April

Conley Kilinski provides analysis that reveals the narrative's subtle sophistication and richness. Framing her argument with "neighborliness" theory, Kilinski asserts that the book's strategically unfolding episodes map the possibility for building and sustaining healthy community. Rounding out the collection, David Brauer's final chapter, "Hatred and Hope in the American South: Rhetorical Excavations in Lillian Smith's *Our Faces, Our Words*," considers Smith's careful rhetorical navigations that balance critique with sympathy, personal with public, and *pathos* with *logos* in the experimental 1964 book. Brauer's argument reveals that even in this exploration of 1960s race dynamics, Smith's writerly approach to life dominated her engagement with subject and reader. Together these studies constitute a rich and rigorous investigation of Smith's contribution to American letters.

Conclusion

Lillian Smith did not write primarily to sell books or impress critics. Her consistent and provocative themes indicate that she was not driven by a desire for fame or wealth. For her, the ability to exercise her artistic talents and link her imagination with ours was not an end in itself but a means to healthier humanity. She wrote in pursuit of a better world, and because she was determined and willing to imagine such a place, she felt honor bound to draw the reader into that process. Her tendency to register her surroundings and her experiences as artists do—observing closely, recording, interpreting, and sharing her artistically represented impressions—yielded writings that rouse readers to consider the world anew. If she was at times guilty of preaching, she was nonetheless true to her own artistic principles. Even in light of harsh criticism, she retained her work's integrity through guileless curiosity, courage, earnestness, and a distinct aesthetic sense. The essays collected here provide new orientation points and broaden the road for readers exploring the landscapes of her writings. As these essays attest, the journey on which

Smith invites us is at times steep and precarious, but that wild region, rendered through her keen poetic sensibility, is one of sublime vistas and valuable self-discovery.

Notes

1. Smith emphasizes the importance of such bridge building in her letter to a teacher, Mr. Hartley, who asked on behalf of his students whether schooling was necessary for good writing. Smith argues that the most important learning and personal development occur beyond the classroom: "And then there is always what you learn when you build bridges to other people: to one, then to one more, and on and on" ("Letter to Mr. Hartley" 15).

2. For more detail about Smith's experience during these years, see Blackwell and Clay 20; Loveland 11–17.

3. The bulk of Smith's papers are held at University of Florida Smathers Libraries and at the University of Georgia's Hargrett Rare Book and Manuscript Library.

4. In their acknowledgments, Gladney and Hodgens recognize their project's debt to Amason and his LES Center board.

Works Cited

Belton, Don. "Lillian Smith: Walking a Trembling Earth." *Hollins Critic*, vol. 20, no. 3, 1983, pp. 1–12.

Blackwell, Louise, and Frances Clay. *Lillian Smith*. Twayne, 1971.

Brantley, Will. *Feminine Sense in Southern Memoir: Smith, Glasgow, Welty, Hellman, Porter, and Hurston*. UP of Mississippi, 1993.

Brewer, Pat B. "Lillian Smith: A Thorn in the Flesh of Crackerdom." *Furman Studies*, vol. 26, 1980, pp. 104–14.

Brinkmeyer, Robert H. "Richard Weaver, Lillian Smith, the South and the World." *The Oxford Handbook of the Literature of the U.S. South*, edited by Fred Hobson and Barbara Ladd, Oxford UP, 2016, pp. 270–89.

Cliff, Michelle, editor. *The Winner Names the Age: A Collection of Writings by Lillian Smith*. Norton, 1978.

Garcia, Jay. "Race, Empire, and Humanism in the Work of Lillian Smith." *Radical History Review*, vol. 101, 2008, pp. 59–80.

Gladney, Margaret Rose, editor. *How Am I to Be Heard? Letters of Lillian Smith*. U of North Carolina P, 1993.

Gladney, Margaret Rose. Preface. Gladney, pp. xiii–xviii.

Gladney, Margaret Rose, and Lisa Hodgens. Introduction. Gladney and Hodgens, pp. 1–3.

Gladney, Margaret Rose, and Lisa Hodgens, editors. *A Lillian Smith Reader*. U of Georgia P, 2016.

Haddox, Thomas F. "Lillian Smith, Cold War Intellectual." *Southern Literary Journal*, vol. 44, no. 2, 2012, pp. 51–68.

Hobson, Fred. *Tell about the South: The Southern Rage to Explain*. Louisiana State UP, 1983.

Jenkins, McKay. "Metaphors of Race and Psychological Damage in the 1940s American South: The Writings of Lillian Smith." *Racing and (E)racing Language: Living with the Color of Our Words*, edited by Ellen J. Goldner and Safiya Henderson-Holmes, Syracuse UP, 2001, pp. 99–123.

Lewis, Nghana Tamu. *Entitled to the Pedestal: Place, Race, and Progress in White Southern Women's Writing, 1920–1945*. U of Iowa P, 2007.

Lillian E. Smith Center. Piedmont College. https://www.piedmont.edu/lillian-smith-center. Accessed January 9, 2019.

Loveland, Anne C. *Lillian Smith, a Southerner Confronting the South: A Biography*. Louisiana State UP, 1986.

Richards, Gary. *Lovers and Beloveds: Sexual Otherness in Southern Fiction, 1936–1961*. Louisiana State UP, 2005.

Robinson, Jo Ann. "Lillian Smith: Reflections on Race and Sex." *Southern Exposure*, vol. 4, no. 4, 1977, pp. 43–48.

Singal, Daniel Joseph. *The War Within: From Victorian to Modernist Thought in the South, 1919–1945*. U of North Carolina P, 1982.

Smith, Lillian. "Children Talking." Gladney and Hodgens, pp. 131–41.

Smith, Lillian. *The Journey*. Forgotten Books, 2018.

Smith, Lillian. *Killers of the Dream*. Norton, 1994.

Smith, Lillian. "Letter to Mr. Hartley." Gladney and Hodgens, pp. 12–16.

Smith, Lillian. Letter to Wilma Dykeman Stokely, October 30, 1965. Gladney, pp. 331–34.

Smith, Lillian. *Memory of a Large Christmas*. U of Georgia P, 1996.

Smith, Lillian. "Novelists Need a Commitment." *Saturday Review*, December 24, 1960, pp. 18–19.

Smith, Lillian. *Now Is the Time*. Dell, 1955.

Smith, Lillian. *One Hour*. U of North Carolina P, 1994.

Smith, Lillian. *Our Faces, Our Words*. Norton, 1964.

Smith, Lillian. "The Role of the Poet in a World of Demagogues." Cliff, pp. 160–65.

Smith, Lillian. *Strange Fruit*. Harcourt, 1944, 1972.

Snelling, Paula. Preface. Cliff, pp. 11–16.

Sosna, Morton. *In Search of the Silent South*. Columbia UP, 1977.

"Lillian Smith." *Southern Literary Trail*. http://www.southernliterarytrail.org/clayton.html. Accessed January 9, 2019.

White, Helen, and Redding S. Sugg Jr. *From the Mountain*. Memphis State UP, 1972.

Yaeger, Patricia. *Dirt and Desire: Reconstructing Southern Women's Writing, 1930–1990*. U of Chicago P, 2000.

CHAPTER 1

Mind Where You Puts Yo Feet: A Study of Southern Boundaries in Lillian Smith's *Strange Fruit*

—*Tanya Long Bennett*

They can't kill you efn dey don strike you. Member dat. Jus mind where you puts yo feet. All of you, you hear!
—Tillie Anderson (*Strange Fruit* 22)

Nonnie, Bess, and Eddie Anderson remember well the lessons they learned from their mother, Tillie, as African American children growing up just outside Maxwell, Georgia, in Black Town. Although when "listening to her words, [they] thrust their roots more firmly into that soil out of which they had come" (23), they also absorb her subtle warnings about where black children can stand and where they cannot.[1] Lillian Smith's 1944 novel *Strange Fruit* boldly explores the taboos of 1920s small-town Georgia life, unveiling the violence that underlies often neurotic relationships within communities like the fictional Maxwell, Georgia, thought to be based on Smith's birthplace, Jasper, Florida. An adamant desegregationist, Smith argued that southern slavery and the Jim Crow laws that followed it had deformed all who participated in them, black as well as white. Further, her vision of a healthier and nobler humanity demanded that *all* social ideologies be continually investigated to avoid similarly dehumanizing dynamics.

Tracing the interactions of Maxwell residents, *Strange Fruit* acknowledges that people desire both a safe and secure home for themselves and their loved ones and the ability to engage freely in the world at large. On the face of it, the two dreams are not mutually exclusive, but, Smith emphasizes, pursuit of these impulses is inevitably complicated by economic and psychological factors that, if not recognized as such, can coalesce into rigid social structures positioning these two goals in opposition to each other. As the novel illustrates, such structures are often perpetuated under the guise of moral and religious codes and as natural law, and the neuroses that shape them are the more dangerous for being hidden and hence unarticulated. In most towns, however, these systems manifest themselves visibly in physical boundaries. Although these boundaries are often accepted, initially, as a way to provide order and stability to human society, they can result in stifling environments that stunt rather than nourish and protect. Under such circumstances, people of the lower castes, such as the black Andersons, as well as higher-status community members like the white Deens, become "strange fruit."

This chapter examines the boundaries of *Strange Fruit*'s fictional Maxwell to better understand the impact of segregation on the lives of the town's inhabitants. On its face, Maxwell appears to be a tightly knit community of good-natured, caring people, living and working together in near harmony; however, viewed as a map, the town reveals systematic "divide and conquer" practices that keep residents in their places, often at the price of their mental well-being and sometimes even of their lives. Middle-class white residential neighborhoods and white-owned downtown businesses serve as the orientation point for the town as a whole, with Black Town homes skirting Maxwell's city limits, alleyways linking the two communities in a symbiotic economic relationship.

Smith's childhood hometown of Jasper sheds some light on the Maxwell that she portrays in the novel. Named after the Revolutionary War veteran William Jasper, the Florida community was settled in the early 1800s by white migrants primarily from Georgia and

A Study of Southern Boundaries in *Strange Fruit*   23

South Carolina, some bringing slaves. For many years, these settlers fought with native Seminoles over the territory, but in 1858, with US government support, the settlers secured their stake, forcing the remaining Seminoles to relinquish the territory and retreat either to Oklahoma reservations or sparsely inhabited Big Cypress swampland. After the Civil War, the Savannah, Florida and Western Railway was completed and a depot built in Jasper just north of the town's center. The economic development that followed gravitated toward the railroad depot, shifting the town's orientation in the direction of commercial activity. While Jasper has survived the Great Depression and other recessions since the 1920s, like other small towns, it has had to negotiate economic challenges such as an interstate highway that bypasses the town rather than drawing travelers into its city limits. The town's official boundaries were expanded in 2000, for example, to incorporate the Hamilton County Correctional Institute in an effort to sustain Jasper's economic viability ("Jasper, Florida"). This small Florida town's cartographic history illuminates the complicated ways that location, civic status, and economic forces can intersect to shape the lives of a region's residents.

Smith's rendering of Maxwell reflects this point powerfully. Central to Maxwell is College Street, where high-status white families live, and on which some run businesses, like the Deens' Corner Drugstore. In the alley behind College Street, the garbage of the stores is piled to preserve clean and tidy storefronts, and the town's black residents generally traverse this parallel "Back Street" rather than College Street's sidewalks. On Back Street, Salamander's offers a lunch counter to black customers who cannot patronize the Deens' drugstore. At the end of Back Street, Brown's Hardware Store and Pug Pusey's Supply Store sit near Maxwell's water tank, and nearby, freight is hauled in and out of the area on trains. Although technically part of White Town, these border areas are characterized by racially mixed commercial interactions that enable a complex economy to function: African American delivery boys come and go, and workers purchase items needed for turpentine farms and lumber mills, money passing through the hands of rich and poor, black and white, alike. On the outer edges of Maxwell lie the town's ball grounds, one for whites and one for blacks. In these male sporting venues, the classes of each race mix more freely than in restaurants, offices, and churches, though black and white men still do not play with or against one another on these grounds.

Walking toward home from town, the Andersons pass the ball fields, the African Methodist Episcopal Church, Evergreen Cemetery—where white dead are buried—then "an ancient row of cedars" (13), and finally the house of the mentally ill, white Miss Ada, before coming to Black Town, the entrance to which is marked by a picket gate. While the home of Miss Ada and her elderly mother is now in a ramshackle state, its situation at the end of the "ancient row of cedars" near the cemetery suggests that her family at one time held a prominent place in the community.

Although Maxwellians not identifying as white do not live in White Town, except in rare cases, there are recognizable class boundaries in Black Town itself. Near the edge of the swamp, both beautiful and haunted, the Andersons live in a run-down two-story house just beyond the picket gate and Miss Ada's house; in fact, Miss Ada watches Bess's son, Jackie, when Bess is working as a maid for the Browns. Since Miss Ada is considered crazy, the townspeople do not find this racial overlap offensive, though many of them do consider the Spelman-educated Anderson sisters "biggety" (1). Farther out of town, we find the Negro Quarters and the mill settlements populated by poor white workers, who often compete with their black counterparts for the manual-labor jobs on farms and mills.

Though Maxwell's borders are relatively fixed during the 1920s time frame of *Strange Fruit*, some movement of whites in Black Town, and vice versa, does occur. The townspeople understand that many white Maxwell men have lovers in Black Town. Middle-class white men generally walk the paths of this section without fear, since their families and white associates often employ the people who live there. Black men and women can walk in College Street and its side neighborhoods, as

A Study of Southern Boundaries in *Strange Fruit*   25

well, but only for work. Each morning, Bess, Nonnie, and other women in maids' uniforms make the trek to the homes in this area to clean house, cook, and take care of white children. As an exception to the rules associated with these geographic markers, Henry McIntosh, who is black, lives in the servants' cabin behind the Deens' big yellow house, as his mother and father did before him. When his parents, Mamie and Ten, faced the decision of whether to leave thirteen-year-old Henry to live in the cabin or take him with them to Baxley to farm cotton, Mamie argued for leaving him with the Deens so that he could go to school. Ten's expression of frustration about the arrangement reveals the unique tensions of living across the line from one's own social group: "Hate livin in Deen's back yard. Told you a hundard time it'd be better in the quarters where we'd be free to do as we like. I don want ma boy brung up wid no white boy—don want none of it!" (113). Yet, attached to the humble abode as the only home he has ever known, and to Tracy Deen as a sort of surrogate brother, Henry stays and remains houseboy to the Deens even after becoming a grown man.

Smith's story of the South's "strange fruit" arises from a plot involving two young lovers, Nonnie Anderson and Tracy Deen. Although Nonnie is pregnant with Tracy's child, he is ultimately unable to sustain his commitment to her in the face of pressures from his family and friends to take the "right path" and marry the esteemed Dorothy Pusey instead (199–200). Out of guilt, Tracy pays his friend-servant Henry to marry Nonnie and, as a result of the insult implied in such a transaction, is shot and killed by Nonnie's infuriated brother Ed. Foreseeing local outrage over the murder of a white man in Black Town, Ed's sister Bess arranges with their friend Sam Perry to get Ed out of town quickly and quietly, and rather than waiting for an investigation or a trial, a white mob of Maxwell locals lynches and burns the easily targeted Henry for the murder. This plot, tracing the movement of black and white characters around and across Maxwell's boundaries, illustrates well how these borders serve both literally and symbolically to determine the paths of the novel's characters and, ultimately, to deform them psychologically.

In *Psychology Comes to Harlem: Rethinking the Race Question in Twentieth-Century America*, Jay Garcia notes that although the lyrics of Billie Holiday's "Strange Fruit" refer to a vigilante hanging, and Smith's novel culminates in a lynching, Smith employed this title to emphasize the deformed "personalities that [result] from 'racist culture'" (117), including vigilantes and onlookers, whites as well as blacks. Investigating the causes of this personality distortion, Garcia recognizes Smith's apt portrayal of "rigid geographical demarcations of the color line" (117), both a reflection of the physical reality of the 1920s South and an effective metaphor for the psychological color line that ruled the lives of southerners, compromising their mental health and their very humanity.

On a globe, Maxwell would not seem to be the center of anything, really. In the southeast corner of the United States, the town's place on the earth is not a common orientation point or destination for travelers. For young men like Ed Anderson and Tracy Deen, fighting in Europe during World War I, the perspective offered from across the Atlantic is enlightening. Ed has, as a result of leaving Maxwell and using his talents for the US government, developed into a confident and dignified man, disdainful of anyone who considers him otherwise. Disgusted by Maxwell's continued segregation and the degradation it causes, he argues that Nonnie should return with him to Washington, DC, to find more dignified work as he has.

Tracy found psychological freedom from Maxwell's inflexible mind-set during his time in France, as well: "Months in the Ruhr Valley left you time to think. Cut off from everything that makes it hard to think at home, it was easier" (48). Here, beyond the mental and behavioral conditioning of Maxwell, he realizes that he is in love with Nonnie, the lovely young black woman that he has known most of his life. His love provides him with a new point by which to orient himself: "He saw her, tender and beautiful, holding in her eyes her pliant spirit, in the movement of her body, her easy right words, low, deep voice, all that gave his life meaning" (50). Back in Maxwell with Nonnie, beginning to feel the tentacles of whiteness tighten around him once more, Tracy proposes, offhandedly, that he and Nonnie might move back to France together, suggesting for Nonnie a new notion of existence: "When he said the word something happened to Nonnie's face and he was startled—as if he had lighted ten thousand candles with one small half-thought-out word" (57).

Nonnie's attachment to Tracy is based, at least in part, on the broadened worldly perspective that the relationship opens up for her. Not only did he protect her from the advances of little white boys when she was a child, but he also talked to her about the world "outside" hers. She strives to describe for Tracy his effect on her: "You told me about the other side of the world—geography—I didn't know a thing about that" (137). Although Tracy flunked out of college, his experience and his understanding of books and ideas, nurtured generously by his parents and teachers, fire Nonnie's imagination in a way that even her Spelman education did not. It is interesting to note that Spelman administrators were upset with Smith at her suggestion, in *Strange Fruit*, that graduates of the historically black college for women might return to their small towns and become servants and, worse, illicit lovers of local white men (Loveland 72). Yet opportunities for Spelman's female graduates were definitely limited in the 1920s, and women like Nonnie and Bess would have faced disproportionate challenges, economic and otherwise, even after obtaining a much-desired college degree. Smith herself noted, defending her portrayal of these characters, "Unfortunately, under a system of segregation and racial discrimination, a college education does not solve the Negro's problems. . . . It is not the full answer to the Negro's problem, and does not, in its present form, solve the white man's problems either" ("Lillian Smith Answers Some Questions about *Strange Fruit*" 128). Nonnie might reasonably consider Tracy's momentary fantasy of taking her back to France with him as a promising possibility for a more fulfilling life. In spite of Tracy's failure to follow through with the idea, his role in providing her a glimpse of unrestricted psychological terrain secures him her devotion. Eileen Boris asserts that *Strange Fruit* "dramatizes not only the ways that segregation perverted bodily integrity, but also how the sexual defined the quest for economic, social, and political rights" (5). Though some critics have expressed disappointment that Nonnie misses the supposed opportunities her degree would offer, she perhaps considers Tracy, albeit subconsciously, as a liaison through whom she could more fully engage with the world.

Ed, Tracy, and Nonnie all imagine a freer existence outside the confines of their Georgia hometown, but Maxwell has a strong hold on the novel's characters. Its centrality to their psychic maps overrides its obscure global position and their desire to escape it. Maxwell is home for them. When Ed expresses dismay that his sisters would stay in this "dump" (31) even after their mother has died, Bess tries to articulate for herself why she does so:

> Moss . . . trailing in your face when you're little . . . you'd make great pillows of it, flop down in them, feeling luxurious and rich. Oak trees you couldn't reach around. . . . Thickets of yellow jessamine . . . and violets . . . fly-catchers in low marshy places, looking so pretty, spreading their yellow fingers through the grass, smelling so bad when you put your nose to them. . . . That's the way you feel about the place where you were born. Always looking for it. Always staying or coming back, searching for the you that you left there. (36–37)

Ed is resolute in his refusal to live in the Georgia town where he grew up, feeling distinctly diminished when he is there. Steven A. Reich describes the Great Black Migration from the rural South to cities such as New York, Chicago, and Washington during and after World War I. "Race was," according to Reich, "obviously the common denominator in determinations to migrate, but motives were often filtered through the gender identities of black men and women. The pernicious characteristics of Jim Crow race relations—disenfranchisement, segregation, and economic marginalization—militated against African American men's claims to the status of manhood as it was defined by the dominant culture" (203). Ed's aversion to Maxwell

A Study of Southern Boundaries in *Strange Fruit*   29

reflects this dynamic. As he faces College Street near the beginning of the novel, "he looked straight into Georgia. White girls in cars blew horns, ordered cokes, laughed, crossed their legs, uncrossed them, stared through him as their line of vision passed his body. He was a black digit marked out by white chalk. He wasn't there on the sidewalk. He had never been there . . . he just wasn't anywhere—where those eyes looked—where those damned eyes—" (8). Yet Bess recognizes that Ed will never fully shake his connection with Maxwell, even after he has shot Tracy and is fleeing for New York: "Even if he were safe, even if he escaped, he'd still have to come back in his mind and look at that white man he'd killed. Sooner or later he would have to do that, and when he did, when he made that journey back, something would happen inside him and it wouldn't be good" (280).

Ed's confusion, the strong pull back to Maxwell juxtaposed against feelings of humiliation associated with the place, reflects gender identity's complication of race and geography.[2] While Ed seeks psychological survival by living in the North, away from the scenes of his childhood, the Andersons' lifelong friend Sam Perry stays in Maxwell, negotiating his manhood daily in and around the town, navigating white-male-dominated spaces to treat his patients. Even his medical degree and his thriving practice do not buy him the right to stand equal to white men of Maxwell, no matter how poor or ignorant they are. When Ed accompanies Sam on his rounds to the Negro Quarters, Sam parks his car out of sight of the white farm owner, Bill Talley. "Better stop here, I reckon," Sam explains to Ed. "Old Talley don't like to see us riding in automobiles. Might as well walk the rest of the way" (164). Self-preservation in this land-scape requires careful mental gymnastics. Sam's deceased wife Ella ostensibly had an affair with a white man, and now he thinks of her, when he allows himself to remember her at all, as something like the accomplice in a theft, attributing to her a "cheapness and nastiness" (33) that he cordons off from himself to protect his self-respect. Yet even in the face of these degrading factors, Sam stays in Maxwell. The alternative would require, as it does for Ed, redrawing his psychological map someplace else, where he would have no familiar landmarks by which to orient oneself.

It is difficult to say whether whiteness or manliness is the more dominant factor of privilege in social structures like Maxwell's, where relatively kind white men like Tom Harris believe that the best way to prevent violence in the area would be to "bring a drove of black women in there [the chain-gang's camp] once a week" (302). While Ed and Sam must avoid even looking at white women and girls or else face consequences as grave as lynching, even white women pay a high price for their access to College Street, trading their sexuality, psychological integrity, and the happiness of their loved ones for status, stability and security. Smith's portrayal of Tracy's mother, Alma, seems at times an outright condemnation of such women, who seem to choke out of their husbands and children their sexual energy, intellectual rigor, and idealism. In *Killers of the Dream*, Smith alleges:

> The majority of [white] southern women convinced themselves that God had ordained that they be deprived of pleasure, and meekly stuffed their hollowness with piety, trying to believe the tightness they felt was hunger satisfied. . . . These women turned away from the ugliness which they felt powerless to cope with and made for themselves and their families what they called a "normal" life. . . . With their gardens and their homes, these women tried to shut out evil, and sometimes succeeded only in sheltering their children from good. (141–42)

Alma Deen has never been able to enjoy even conjugal sex, disgusted by bodily fluids and smells, even those of her own children. Aside from Henry McIntosh's lynching, Alma's willingness to sacrifice Tracy's happiness for the sake of the family's social position seems one of the most intentional and brutal applications of White Town's strict code. She seems to have embraced her social role willingly, though her own mother's discouragement of intellectual pursuits did limit Alma's choices. She ended up marrying Tut Deen soon after he completed medical school; when he "asked her to marry him, it was for Alma

A Study of Southern Boundaries in *Strange Fruit* 31

as if someone had opened a gate which led down a faraway road" (75). Her ambition has sharpened her edges, making her formidable even to her own husband and children. Yet one telltale remnant of the Alma who existed before coming to Maxwell is her wish for her daughter Laura to earn a PhD and teach in a university, though it would mean Laura's settling away from home. This notion evidences Alma's understanding, on some level, that Maxwell's boundaries ultimately strangle the humanity out of even women like herself. Not only does her role preclude sexuality and philosophical integrity, but she must serve as the scapegoat of men like her own husband, who thinks of her as an immovable cow, though she has to a great extent held together his medical practice and household all their married life. The wife of the wealthy landowner Cap'n Rushton plays a similar role, serving as his connection to "town," enabling him to skirt the confines of Maxwell's mores and simultaneously reap the benefits of his position in its society. Even Bess is blamed, by both Ed and Sam, for the stifling effect of her caretaking, even as they take advantage of it.

This complicated tangle of perpetrator and victim, insider and outsider, confirms Smith's assertion that no one in such a system goes unscathed: all suffer psychological damage as a result. And although crossing the Mason-Dixon Line appeals to Ed and many other African Americans tired of navigating geographies such as Maxwell's, leaving may not lead to the desired healing. Johnson and Michaelsen explain, "Identities don't travel well. They don't work well abroad . . . ; and home, too, is always foreign, always on the other side of the border" (20). Further, Ed's expectation of opportunity for Nonnie in the North carries some naïveté, since her gender would undoubtedly factor into her experience there, as it has for him. Dynamics of mobility are complicated by the notion of "gendered places," for example. Unlike Tracy or Ed, Nonnie is not more likely to find safety and security in the North than in the South if she does not understand the codes embedded in its particular and complex environments. Rachel Silvey explains, in "Geographies of Gender and Migration: Spatializing Social Difference," that women are often "othered" at night or in "public" places. . . . The structures of gender, race, and class play into determining whose bodies belong where, how different social groups subjectively experience various environments (e.g., who feels safe in "public" places, powerful in alleyways, at home in red-light districts, afraid in the suburbs, or "in place" in the central city), and what sorts of exclusionary and disciplinary techniques are applied to specific bodies. (70)

In light of such conditions, the choice of Alma, Bess, Laura, and Nonnie to stay in Maxwell may be founded on logic beyond an attachment to "home." Silvey argues, for example, that "if African-American women can use their spatial rootedness in a community to their advantage, this suggests that pre-given conceptions of mobility as power and immobility as oppression require further investigation" (65).

That Lillian Smith herself chose to live and work in the South, while caring for aging parents and running the girls' camp her father had founded, parallels *Strange Fruit*'s implication that finding a path to healing may require rooting out the problem from within. Although "whiteness theory" is relatively young as a tool for addressing racism, Smith alleges in *Now Is the Time* (1955) that white people as a social class are "arrogant in our overestimation of whiteness" (72). That she labels whiteness as a sociopolitical position in this treatise marks a crucial step in the process of disrupting white domination. The territory of "White Town" is rarely named aloud in the novel, thus revealing much about the kinds of boundaries that rule Maxwell. Johnson and Michaelsen use the term "soft borders" to refer to unofficial geographical lines like the ones marking White Town, as well as ideological boundaries like "benevolent nationalism" and "cultural essentialism" (1). The boundaries that sustain Maxwell's order are certainly "soft" in this sense. Except for Tracy Deen, who spends a good deal of time in Black Town visiting Nonnie, the only characters who use the term "White Town" to identify that privileged space are those who cannot move freely in it. Ruth Frankenberg elaborates on the relationship between space and race in such a system: "Whiteness is a location of

A Study of Southern Boundaries in *Strange Fruit*   33

structural advantage, of race privilege. . . . It is a 'standpoint,' a place from which white people look at ourselves, at others, at society" (1). One effect of standing inside this space is a failure to recognize it as a space, though the privileged will quickly resort to violence to protect that space if its borders are breached. The power associated with this territory is twofold: first, it is the relatively richly resourced "home" in which whites play out the daily dynamics necessary to sustaining privileged life; but more importantly, in its namelessness, it is surrounded by an invisible psychological barbed-wire fence that gouges outsiders ignorant enough to pass too close to it.

Sam Perry understands well the double-edged threat of this barbed wire. Dedicated to serving his fellow black community members, and to preserving a peaceful relationship with the white community to do so, Sam must contend with the blindness of his white counterparts to the violence that their position generates. When he goes to Tom Harris to warn him that the mob will be coming for Henry McIntosh to kill him for Tracy's murder, Sam notes internally, "Trouble about going to white folks, they always think you're exaggerating" (333). Sure enough, although Tom knows that black workers periodically "disappear" out at Bill Talley's farm, Tom's response to the seasoned physician's warning is to downplay the danger: "No, they won't get him. Haven't had a lynching here in ten years. We're not having one today" (338). Likely based on Smith's own father, Harris is portrayed as one of the most sympathetic white businessmen in the Maxwell area, taking some pains to treat workers equally and humanely. But his desire to believe in the benevolence of his fellow white neighbors obscures evidence to the contrary, and he becomes angry at Sam for pressing the issue: "You've forgot, Sam, . . . there're things no nigger on earth can say to a white man!" (342). Harris does, eventually, follow up on Sam's warnings, driving to the white ball field to intervene in the mob's activities, but because of his initial hesitation, he is too late to prevent the lynching and burning of the innocent man. Only his own children are willing to acknowledge aloud the part of "upstanding" white Maxwell citizens in Henry's death. Harriet asserts,

"I've always wondered how a lyncher feels.... Now I know.... Every Southerner knows, of course. We lynch the Negro's soul every day of our lives" (355).

Valerie Babb clarifies how refusing to consider whiteness from *inside* the barbed wire perpetuates race ideology, even as those outside it are publicly examining their wounds:

> The resistance to naming white privilege and the scholarly silence that has precluded the analysis of this racial category are the result of whiteness being presumed the norm. In contrast, racial constructs commonly identified as aberrant, exotic, or Other have been named and explored, precisely because being deemed valid in a culture that seeks to marginalize them necessitates articulation and assessment. (15)

Babb's point here is well-taken: while the residents of Black Town are aware of their disadvantage and consciously consider ways to regain their full humanity, including economic opportunity and psychological health, it is the guardians of White Town who continue to police the borders (to a great extent subconsciously) and hence sustain the system that deforms not only residents of color but also themselves. Smith's portrayal of the community implies that any position of privilege over others requires destructive betrayal—not only of the "other" but also of one's own values and psychological wholeness. The most obvious example of this expensive purchase is Tracy's betrayal of Nonnie. While it seems, early in the novel, that Tracy will give up his place in White Town to honor his love for Nonnie, he ultimately cannot withstand the pressures of his mother, Preacher Dunwoodie, and the white community at large to do otherwise. Not only does Tracy succumb to the attraction of economic security, in the shape of farmland offered by his father, but Tracy's desire to be accepted by his "home" community of White Town is so strong that he allows his very self to be mutilated.

The mechanism that ultimately "breaks" Tracy is the message of chauvinistic Christianity being spouted by Preacher Dunwoodie at

A Study of Southern Boundaries in *Strange Fruit*

the town revival, which notably is held on the same lot where the circus performs when it comes to Maxwell. Dunwoodie first seduces Tracy by welcoming him into the brotherhood of men, distinctly separate from and superior to women. Although the preacher states that it is women, mothers in particular, who best represent God's love, he appeals to Tracy's sexual identity to establish their shared masculinity, telling the opening of a risqué joke about an unfaithful wife and trailing off tantalizingly (89). The preacher asserts that Tracy can best reap the benefits of a relationship with God if he unfetters himself from "woman's world": "Women teach us to love the Lord, and our children, and then *we* build the churches, don't we, and *we* keep them going. Sure. Just as we make the living for the children, we do the farming, we create the cities. We do the work. Sure. That's right" (89). Further developing his strategy to draw Tracy into the fold, the preacher begins aligning this sense of manhood with whiteness: "You see, Deen, you have to keep pushing them back across that nigger line. Keep pushing! . . . God made the white race for a great purpose" (88). Although Tracy is resistant to Preacher Dunwoodie's brand of Christianity, he finds himself disoriented after this talk. He seeks out Nonnie to clear his head, "but the moment he opened the screen door of his house and entered that hall, things changed as if he had found his sense of direction out in the swamp—and lost it again" (97). Dunwoodie's rhetoric, leading Tracy toward alignment with Maxwell's power structures, is seductive, effective as both a plot device and a metaphor for the insidiousness of racism.

"Across the business section of town" from Salamander's (216) and set up on the lot where "Ringling's Circus [is held] each winter" (248), the revival tent is a strange and powerful place. Tracy remembers Preacher Dunwoodie as an acrobat himself: "Once you'd seen him, years ago when he was here, illustrate his text by climbing the pole of the big tent" (82). Though blacks and whites are segregated in the tent, all Maxwellians are urged to attend the revival services. The singing of the congregation can be heard across White Town and out into Black Town. The revival is supported by the wealthiest families because, as Alma explains to her daughter Laura, "This isn't only a revival in our church. It's a community project. While some things may seem a little old-fashioned or unnecessary from our point of view, all of Maxwell has not had your opportunities. Brother Dunwoodie has a message people need, educated or uneducated. It is especially those poor mill people who do need God" (66). Alma takes seriously her responsibility in helping perpetuate this kind of Christianity to sustain the existing social order, and both she and Preacher Dunwoodie understand that money invested in this mechanism will pay off in preserving the status quo. Dunwoodie preaches on "Christian Stewardship" (248), with the understanding that "however many mill people were converted, a revival could not be called a success in Maxwell until the prominent citizens, some of whom had drifted away from the church, were returned to the fold" (249). Zealously pressing the notion that God brings prosperity to the faithful, Dunwoodie salves the consciences of the townspeople who benefit most from Maxwell's segregation, even as he pressures them for donations. Further, if God blesses his own, the subtle message to poor whites is that to identify oneself as "unblessed" is to equate oneself with the lowly, the tainted, the "cheap and nasty." Better to reap minimal benefit from an ideology privileging whites than to challenge that ideology and risk falling to the very back of the privilege line. Dunwoodie understands that the need for self-respect is almost as strong as hunger.

That the lynching and this revival meeting both occur on the edge of Maxwell at the climax of the novel is no surprise. If the community's pecking order seems to be threatened by blacks' earning college degrees, joining the army, and moving North for better-paying jobs, the pressure building in Maxwell finds its release valves in this liminal space on the edge of town. The mob of angry whites, who feel that they would lose footing in not getting just payment for a white man's murder, catch up to their scapegoat Henry on the whites' ball field, near the water tower. The unspoken and hence powerful white identity of the county can be observed gathering its forces, asserting its unspoken dominance:

A Study of Southern Boundaries in *Strange Fruit*   37

Down the sand roads of the county they had come. Bill and Dee, and the others. From Sug Rushton's turpentine farm, and the cotton fields . . . from Harris's sawmill . . . from a shanty back of Shaky Pond . . . and Ellatown . . . from Old Cap'n Rushton's commissary, and the logging camp. Roads threading whitely through the county, curving around oak-black lake and pond, pushing across swamp and hammock, tying its cotton and little grayed cabins, its barrels of rosin and its turpentine and tall pines, mule and church and bank, white folks and black, to Maxwell, and to each other. Down these roads they came, shadows falling foreshortened and stuffy on palmetto clumps as they plodded along in the heat, hearts as slashed as the pines under which they paused now and then, bodies as drained as the sand on their feet. But white. God-white and immaculate. . . . And now they were on their way to put the nigger in his place. (328)

Smith's penetrating portrayal of Maxwell's physical and psychological boundaries generates a clear and disturbing map in the imaginations of her readers. Recognizing the familiar and seemingly idyllic ambience of small-town southern life in the pages of *Strange Fruit*, readers must also confront here the "soft" but brutal borders that control and ultimately dehumanize all the town's residents. Smith's determination to offer us this view reflects her optimism, even as it is driven by her fierce insistence that we see and acknowledge the ugliness in common human behaviors. Elaborating on this optimism, Thomas F. Haddox notes that Smith held a "secularized vision of Christian brotherhood" that was grounded in her belief in "a universal human nature" (51). He writes that according to Smith, "above all . . . 'the race/sex/sin spiral' endemic to southern culture . . . poisoned otherwise spontaneous and healthy relationships" (51). In his portrait of Smith as a Cold War intellectual, Haddox emphasizes her belief that true social change would come not through intellectual or political revolution but "as the sum of individual awakenings, as oppressors and oppressed discover their mutual humanity and learn to form constructive relationships" (51). In *Strange Fruit*, Smith artfully employs multiple points of view, which shift strategically to reveal unfamiliar and unacknowledged perspectives to readers, regardless of their color, class, or gender. In doing so, she guides us through the various territories in and around Maxwell. Walking these areas as Smith's characters—white and black, male and female, rich and poor—opens our eyes to Maxwell's markers and lines, even those that are usually invisible. Smith's use of narrative point of view to effect individual awakenings aligns with research indicating that fiction can diminish perceived race boundaries. In a 2014 study, Johnson, Huffman, and Jasper found that through fictional narratives, "basic processes of race perception and emotion perception are modified in ways consistent with prejudice reduction" (88). From our seats in 2021, as we reflect on *Strange Fruit*, as well as on the civil rights movement and other developments and setbacks that have occurred since the novel's publication in 1944, we can see the ongoing need to explore factors of segregation politics and their dynamics. Smith's narrative mapping suggests that understanding geographies and their role in social dynamics takes an important step toward a better-integrated, healthier society.

Notes

1. In this study, I indicate "black" and "white" as race categories in lowercase letters rather than as proper nouns through capitalization. In this rhetorical decision, I am aware of the debates surrounding these terms in the context of race discussion. Beginning "Black" with a capital letter usually indicates respect for an identity and culture long denied the respect and recognition it deserves. Treating "Black" as a proper noun, however, seems to necessitate doing the same with "White." Capitalizing both terms would acknowledge US culture's obsession with race identity, and additionally it would be a gesture of *naming* the whiteness long treated as *non*race, or the norm, in American culture. However, writing "White" (for me, a white scholar) risks enacting a reassertion of the dominance that white America has long imposed on people of color. Because of the complicated and even contradictory meanings associated with these choices, this study uses lowercase for both terms, partly to reduce the distraction that constant repetition of capitalized terms would generate, and partly to acknowledge the humanity of all of Smith's characters, regardless of race.

A Study of Southern Boundaries in *Strange Fruit* 39

2. For a brilliant examination of how southern black writers complicate and disrupt the black/white binary of southern spaces, see Thadious M. Davis's *Southscapes: Geographies of Race, Region, and Literature*. If Smith's portrayal of black characters falls short, it is only in her inability to imagine the resilience possible through a commonly occurring "black space of articulation" (Davis 72).

Works Cited

Babb, Valerie. *Whiteness Visible: The Meaning of Whiteness in American Literature and Culture*. New York UP, 1998.

Boris, Eileen. "'Arm in Arm': Racialized Bodies and Colored Lines." *Journal of American Studies*, vol. 35, 2001, pp. 1–20.

Davis, Thadious M. *Southscapes: Geographies of Race, Region, and Literature*. U of North Carolina P, 2011.

Frankenberg, Ruth. *White Women, Race Matters: The Social Construction of Whiteness*. U of Minnesota P, 1993.

Garcia, Jay. *Psychology Comes to Harlem: Rethinking the Race Question in Twentieth-Century America*. Johns Hopkins UP, 2012.

Haddox, Thomas F. "Lillian Smith, Cold War Intellectual." *Southern Literary Journal*, vol. 44, no. 2, 2012, pp. 51–68.

"Jasper, Florida." Wikipedia, https://en.wikipedia.org/wiki/Jasper,_Florida. Accessed February 3, 2019.

Johnson, Dan R., Brandie L. Huffman, and Danny M. Jasper. "Changing Race Boundary Perception by Reading Narrative Fiction." *Basic and Applied Social Psychology*, vol. 36, no. 1, 2014, pp. 86–90.

Johnson, David E., and Scott Michaelsen. "Border Secrets: An Introduction." *Border Theory: The Limits of Cultural Politics*, edited by Scott Michaelsen and David E. Johnson, U of Minnesota P, 1997, pp. 1–42.

Loveland, Anne C. *Lillian Smith, a Southerner Confronting the South: A Biography*. Louisiana State UP, 1986.

Reich, Steven A. *The Great Black Migration: A Historical Encyclopedia of the American Mosaic*. Greenwood, 2014.

Silvey, Rachel. "Geographies of Gender and Migration: Spatializing Social Difference." *International Migration Review*, vol. 40, no. 1, 2006, pp. 64–81.

Smith, Lillian. *Killers of the Dream*, 1949. Norton, 1994.

Smith, Lillian. *Now Is the Time*. Viking, 1955.

Smith, Lillian. "Lillian Smith Answers Some Questions about *Strange Fruit*." *A Lillian Smith Reader*, edited by Margaret Rose Gladney and Lisa Hodgens, U of Georgia P, 2016, pp. 126–30.

Smith, Lillian. *Strange Fruit*. Harcourt, 1944.

CHAPTER 2

Ghosts of Our Fathers: Rewriting the South in Lillian Smith's *Killers of the Dream*

—Justin Mellette

The realm of autobiography has long provided southerners the opportunity to assess and evaluate the peculiar complexity of their lives, as well as the factors peculiarly endemic to the relationship between the South and America at large. As Fred Hobson observed in his seminal *Tell about the South*, southerners have long held firm to a belief in the significance of their "uniqueness," a mind-set forged by an insistence that the South "is the only American region to have been a separate nation, the only region to have suffered military defeat on its own soil and to have withstood occupation and reconstruction by the enemy. The South has been and remains the most homogeneous of regions, the most provincial, the most insular—and, until recently, the most insecure" (9–11). The "southernness" of this particular ideology is in fact heightened by its overlooking of displaced Native Americans and the legacy of slavery and is in many ways emblematic of the very type of autobiography that a radical like Lillian Smith would come to combat and rebut. Such works, as we will see, imply that southernness—especially southern whiteness—is universal and unassailable, though a closer examination reveals that in fact these claims are ultimately ineffective at hiding the anxious paternalism and fear of the encroaching changes fought for during the civil rights era. And in Smith's subversive and distinct autobiographical work *Killers of the Dream*, she works to combat the pervasive racism of southern culture, shaping her narrative as a rhetorical response to William Alexander Percy's sentimental *Lanterns on the Levee*, among other southern autobiographies of the time (5–6).

The 1940s marked a curious decade in southern letters, as new voices like Richard Wright, Carson McCullers, and Flannery O'Connor broached territory not always covered by dominant (usually white and male) figures such as William Faulkner and Thomas Wolfe in earlier years. In addition to the important work in matters of race, gender, and disability representations in texts, this decade is curiously rich in autobiographical remembrances and considerations of the era, as a variegated selection of authors tackled a breadth of social concerns, many of which stood in opposition to traditional southern culture. Hobson notes that the southern bent toward regionalist writing is presaged in part on anxiety and repression: "To some psychologists amateur and professional the South has been a neurotic society, one that repressed its true feelings about the Negro and constructed defense mechanisms to conceal its guilt over slavery" (11). When examining autobiographical texts, we can further break down the too-long held notion of a southern monolith and parse out the ways in which the signifier "southern" has been associated with an overly broad and totalizing view of the region and its inhabitants, as writers like Smith seek to portray the racism of the time as outlandish, insidious, and worthy of disruption.

Enter Lillian Smith, whose *Killers of the Dream* (1949) functions as an imaginative autobiographical remembrance, yet one that often eschews precise descriptions of Smith's own life in favor of a representative and emblematic pastiche of southern life. Most significantly, the genre fluidity grants Smith the opportunity to finesse her rhetorical engagement with the nostalgic school of memoir, as well as provide perhaps her work's most enduring legacy, its forward-looking optimism, where southerners shifted from an entrenched defiance toward the then-burgeoning civil rights movements into a new paradigm of both racial tolerance and a rejection of the myths that had, in Smith's reckoning, been so damaging to the southern psyche. This optimism ultimately proves surprising, as much of Smith's work is dedicated to exploding the nostalgic world championed by the likes of William Alexander Percy and instead presenting the South as a tortured hellscape. In this dystopia, white supremacy was damaging not only to its most obvious victims, black men and women, but also to those who perpetrated the violence and their less obvious victims, particularly exploited poor whites and southern women, the latter of whom had been placed on pedestals of supposed purity that proved psychologically damaging in their fundamental hypocrisy. Throughout the work, Smith positions herself in opposition to the others writing about the South at this time; in a chapter titled "The Stolen Future," for example, she includes a menagerie of defensive quotes drawn from the likes of Percy, Richard Russell, and Cole Blease. Smith asks readers, "Why can words such as these, which our politicians use whenever the issue of civil rights comes up, stir such anxiety in men's hearts?" (79). Although this moment occurs well into the text, it provides a useful starting point in summarizing Smith's mission, an in-depth look at the process of indoctrination and inculcation that warps the ways in which southerners view race and sexuality, leading up to an idea of white southern exceptionalism that teeters on a razor's edge, always precarious and always threatened.

While *Killers of the Dream* was not necessarily penned as the direct rebuttal of a particular publication, Smith's keen awareness of the writings of her contemporaries is clear. Contextualizing Smith alongside various southern nonfiction writers of her time reveals how striking and progressive her work is in relation to that of her contemporaries. Further, it illuminates her rhetorical prowess in using context to shape her work. William Percy's *Lanterns* provided a useful oppositional springboard for her psychological study of the South through her personal story.

While I focus here primarily on the relationship between *Killers* and sentimental autobiography like Percy's, I should note that *Killers* owes its origin in part to W. J. Cash's book-length treatise *The Mind of the South* (1941), adapted from his earlier article of the same name (a chapter of which was published in Smith's magazine *Pseudopodia* in 1936). The work has been cited by both contemporaneous critics and recent scholars for its significance in defining the South, with much attention to his opening pronouncement, "There exists among us—both North and South—a profound conviction that the South is another land, sharply differentiated from the rest of the American nation, and exhibiting within itself a remarkable homogeneity" (xix). And while the work often discusses southerners in a somewhat reductive manner, it still functions as a useful document of its time for showing the types of stigmatization and denigration of some groups of southerners that a writer like Smith would ultimately decry in her work (xii).[1]

Like *Killers*, Cash's work is not a memoir in any traditional sense but rather a historical and sociological document; perhaps most important to any discussion of Lillian Smith's work, Cash's text provides the types of ruminations on southern life—particularly regarding poor southerners—that blur the boundaries between myth and reality and likely encouraged Smith's own attempt at writing a book-length consideration of the region. Much of the rhetorical prowess of *Killers* stems from the fact that Smith, unlike Cash, resorts to a more personal rather than reportorial tone in her work. At the outset, Cash differentiates between the plantation aristocracy and the poor white; of the former, he writes, "They dwelt in large and stately mansions, preferably white and with columns and Grecian entablature. Their estates were feudal baronies, their slaves quite too numerous ever to be counted, and their social life a thing of Old World splendor and delicacy," one that was "dominated by ideals of honor and chivalry and noblesse—all those sentiments and values and habits of action which used to be, especially in Walter Scott, invariably assigned to the gentleman born and the Cavalier" (xxi). In a passage worth quoting at length, Cash then describes poor whites:

Beneath these was a vague race lumped together indiscriminately as the poor whites—very often, in fact, as the "white-trash." These people belonged in the main to a physically inferior type, having sprung for the most part from the convict servants, redemptioners, and debtors of old Virginia and Georgia, with a sprinkling of the most unsuccessful sort of European peasants and farm laborers and the dregs of the European town slums. And so, of course, the gulf between them and the master classes was impassable, and their ideas and feelings did not enter into the make-up of the prevailing Southern civilization. (xxi)

Cash offers these distinct portraits as a means of combating what he deems as "legends" that ultimately "bear little relation to reality," and he goes to lengths to combat some of these ideals, all the more significant in that his work shares a publication year with William Percy's book-length apologia for the Old South and its way of life (xxii).

This reminder of Cash's rhetorical style and its relationship to Smith's work illustrates the significant work done during this particular moment in southern letters and sets the stage for the distinct contribution Smith would make with *Killers* at the end of the decade. Indeed, she also noted later in life what seems a sense of indebtedness to Cash; in 1965, Smith explained that after the publication of *Killers*, she wrote Alfred Knopf about Cash, stating, "After *Killers*, I had this decent, if quixotic notion, that I should push Cash's book." Yet she also adds that unlike her own work, Cash's work "appeals to the moderates," and it was "not in any sense a 'mind of the South'; it was actually a social history of the old South and its values and communal attitudes. But there was no in-depth probing in that book; the man wasn't capable of such, too sick himself, too involved with his own taboos to dare handle it the way I did" (letter to George Brockway, *How Am I to Be Heard?* 323). Even in discussing a somewhat similarly minded individual like Cash, Smith's desire to differentiate herself from the voices of her (generally male) contemporaries shines through in her correspondence. Indeed, critics have long noted this desire as one of her key contributions to southern literature; Margaret Rose Gladney notes that Smith "entered the public arena as a writer in opposition to the Agrarians" (xiii–xiv). Regarding her critique of "moderates" in the letter about Cash, Smith's lack of patience for milquetoast reactions to racism is well-documented; in a 1948 letter to the *New York Times*, she opens with the sharp rejoinder, "As a southern woman, I am deeply shocked that our liberals are putting up no real fight for human rights in the South" (*How* 119). And in addition to her noted work as editor and director of the Laurel Falls Camp, Smith clearly envisioned herself as a writer and activist that defied simple classification, and one who charted out a career with a keen eye for the prevailing literary atmosphere of the time. Indeed, as early as 1940, she began plans for a book-length southern work akin to Cash's upcoming work; in a 1940 letter to George Reynolds requesting a renewal of the Julius Rosenwald Fellowship, she discusses plans for a book: "There are few spots on the globe as interesting as the South; and perhaps none so rich in startlingly poignant paradoxes . . . Jefferson and Jim Crow . . . madonna and mulatto . . . church-steeple and noose. . . . The last decade and a half has seen the first wide-spread attempts, even by historians and sociologists, to disentangle myth from actuality" (*How Am I* 38). While this work was not fully completed, *Killers of the Dream* is arguably a more unique and fascinating outcome than she envisioned, as it offers not a complete social history per se but rather an emblematic psychological portrait, one that Smith called "the hardest of all books for me to write; it stirred deep and dangerous memories" (qtd. in Gladney 115). In spite of its shortcomings, *The Mind of the South* inspired Smith to employ personal perspective in service of persuasive autobiography.

Just as important, however, is the oppositional rhetoric Smith crafts in *Killers of the Dream*, and William Percy's *Lanterns on the Levee* offers a useful context for this strategy, as Percy's book works to instill a belief in a collective southern memory, albeit one that clearly hierarchizes and critiques certain segments of society. In some admittedly superficial ways, William Percy and Lillian Smith's lives bear certain similarities: each was born to a well-to-do southern family, both understood that literature could serve revolutionary purposes in (re)imagining southern culture, and both hid their homosexuality from a less-than-tolerant surrounding world. Yet, whereas Smith's career was one of combativeness and yearning for future progress, Percy's work is an entrenched account of resisting the shifting tides of civil rights and southern culture. From the opening lines of the foreword, Percy makes evident the idea that *Lanterns on the Levee* will embrace sentiment and nostalgia; he begins with the maudlin declaration, "The desire to reminisce arises not so much I think from the number of years you may happen to have accumulated as from the number of those who meant most to you in life who have gone on the long journey" (n.p.). He asserts from the beginning that his work will consider his understanding of what the South has lost since the Civil War: "So while the world I know is crashing to bits, and what with the noise and the cryings-out no man could hear a trumpet blast, much less an idle evening reverie, I will indulge a heart beginning to be fretful by repeating to it the stories it knows and loves of my own country and my own people" (n.p.). A key consideration of the text will be just how Percy chooses to define his "country" and "people"; though at first it may seem he invokes the South and southerners in a totalizing fashion, as the work progresses, it becomes apparent that Percy's worldview is strongly hierarchical. As Benjamin Wise notes in his biography of Percy, his "self-acceptance and love of place coexisted with his prejudice and conceit. He shared a sense of racial and class superiority with other aristocratic white people" (8). In this manner, one friendly to his perceived audience, we see the first fundamental distinctions between Percy's rendition of the South and the broader discussion and ideals championed by Smith. In the first line of the memoir proper, Percy claims, "My country is the Mississippi Delta, the river country," which immediately demarcates a specific section of the South as warranting attention, important to note lest readers believe that Percy is attempting to comment on the South as a homogeneous entity (though, at times, Percy does approach such a mind-set) (3).

Yet if this indication of humility suggests Percy's hesitation to speak as an authority on the South at large, it is a disingenuous rhetorical move. On the particularity of Mississippi, William Andrews remarks, "Mississippi recognized selfhood not as a function of the subject but of the object, namely the racial other, whose looming presence dictated the need for self-differentiation," and, indeed, much of *Lanterns* deals with Percy's self-fashioning as a benevolent aristocrat (50).

One of Percy's key strategies in establishing himself as a member of the southern gentility is his attempt at outlining racial difference and, specifically, creating distance between himself and the racial other. Thus, from the outset, Percy stands as a far cry from Smith's more pointed critique of the hypocrisy behind so many black-white sexual relationships, the "ghost stories" of the South that illustrate how a racist and supremacist mind-set is used to inculcate hierarchies of paternalism among white southern youth. As Percy's text progresses, it also becomes clear that various groups of whites, particularly poor whites, are sources of consternation and anxiety for Percy. Bertram Wyatt-Brown summarizes the memoir as Percy's attempt to "keep alive a South of plantation ease and perfect decorum that had never really existed," a task clearly at odds with his contemporaries writing "modernistic psychological realism" about the region (14). These dual concerns of Percy's—invoking plantation nostalgia and dispersing blacks and poor whites—are intimately related; Smith herself explores racism as, in part, a tool used by upper-class whites to instill class hierarchies. Percy's linking of aristocracy and obliviousness to the true terrors of slavery, then, is not surprising when considered through Smith's more complex worldview. Yet his failure to analyze the phenomenon critically stands out against Smith's radicalism. In his opening chapter, Percy is decidedly uncritical of slavery in its first mention: "Such was my country hardly more than a hundred years ago. It was about then that slavery became unprofitable in the older Southern states and slave-holders began to look for cheap fertile lands farther west that could feed the many black mouths dependent on them" (5). Percy's sympathies—here as elsewhere—lie with white aristocrats, not the men and women who toiled under slavery, as he mentions that westward expansion was due to the need to feed blacks who were "dependent" on whites. A few pages later he adds, "When the effect of the Emancipation Proclamation was realized by the slaves, they became restless, unruly, even dangerous" (9). Again, Percy emphasizes blacks' threatening status to whites rather than the importance of their liberation. A similar example occurs later when Percy reflects on Reconstruction-era politics, lauding local white men who "bore the brunt of the Delta's fight against scalawaggery and Negro domination during reconstruction, who stole the ballot-boxes which, honestly counted, would have made every county official a Negro, who had helped shape the Constitution of 1890, which in effect and legally disfranchised the Negro" (68–69). And lest readers garner the wrong impression from the sepia-tinted opening pages, he is quick to offer a reminder of the supposed hardships his class faced on account of its smaller size:

> I may seem to have implied that all Delta citizens were aristocrats traveling luxuriously up and down the river or sitting on the front gallery, a mint julep in one hand and a palm-leaf fan in the other, protected from mosquitoes by the smudge burning in the front yard. If so, I have misinterpreted my country. The aristocrats were always numerically in the minority; with the years they have not increased. (16)

In attempting to evoke sympathy for his class, Percy implies that a rising, as yet unnamed, class of whites is threatening this nostalgic past ideal.

As we move toward Smith's response, it is worth noting just how fragile Percy's presentation of whiteness is, as his memories about his own relationships with black people left him vexed and anxious. *Lanterns on the Levee* is noted for Percy's racial paternalism, represented in moments such as his declaration, "I would say to the Negro: before demanding to be a white man socially and politically, learn to be a white man morally and intellectually—and to the white man: the black man is our brother, a younger brother, not adult, not disciplined, but tragic, pitiful, and lovable; act as his brother and be patient" (309). Percy reveals that this patronizing attitude is inculcated from birth (an idea that Smith would actually not disagree with, though she remains far more introspective and critical of this reality); in an early chapter about his childhood, Percy offers the dictum, "Any little boy who was not raised with little Negro children might just as well not have been raised at all" (46). His reminiscence is tinged with nostalgia as he refers to Skillet, his "first-boon companion," as "the best crawfisher in the world," adding "and I was next" (46). Again, the sepia-toned memory and joyful recollection are not surprising; as Benjamin Wise notes, "Percy's memory illuminates not only Percy's identification with and love of black people; it also demonstrates a psychological conceit necessary for the maintenance of segregation: blacks were fit for childhood companionship but not for adult political equality" (33). Wise's point is well-taken, especially in light of Percy's lengthy defense of the segregated southern social structure:

> The righteous are usually in a dither over the deplorable state of race relations in the South. I, on the other hand, am usually in a condition of amazed exultation over the excellent state of race relations in the South. It is incredible that two races, centuries apart in emotional and mental discipline, alien in physical characteristics, doomed by ward and the Constitution to a single, not a dual, way of life, and to an impractical and unpracticed theory of equality which deludes and embitters, heckled and misguided by pious fools from the North and impious fools from the South—it is incredible, I insist, that two such dissimilar races should live side by side with so little friction, in such comparative peace and amity. (286–87)

This passage merits quoting at length to showcase just how much ink Percy is willing to spill to argue for the existence of congenial race relations; the author doth protest too much, indeed. Again, he emphasizes white superiority, calling blacks centuries behind in mental discipline (read, intelligence), referring to equality as "impractical." Though he states that "in the South every white man worth calling white or a man is owned by some Negro, whom he thinks he owns, his weakness and solace and incubus," Percy's rationale for doing so is not to stress a belief in equality but rather to reemphasize his claims that blacks are a mental burden to their white peers in the South, and genteel whites like himself will somehow be forced to care for and paternalistically usher blacks into a new era (287).

Revisiting Percy's memoir serves to remind us of the southern literary context of the time, and understanding the conservatism and nostalgia that Percy champions is pivotal in regarding *Killers of the Dream* as an oppositional text to this line of southern defensiveness. In the chapter titled "The Stolen Future," Smith includes a menagerie of defensive quotes about the South, penned by the likes of Percy as well as other conservatives, including Richard Russell and Cole Blease. From Percy's work, she includes his bloviations on the black man's needing to "be a white man morally," and others where Percy bemoans blacks' failure to assimilate. Smith then asks readers, "How can one idea like segregation become so hypnotic a thing that it binds a whole people together," and urges readers to combat this pervasive mind-set (79). Thus much of *Killers of the Dream*'s oppositional power lies in its carefully crafted countering of *Lanterns* and other sentimental autobiographies of the period.

While *Killers* may not have been written as a direct response to *Lanterns*, at least in the manner that, say, Sutton Griggs's *The Hindered Hand* was a response to Thomas Dixon's pro-Klan racist screeds, Smith's tone and the overall organization of her work, from the dedication through its conclusions, reveal that Percy's voice looms over the text, a ghostly reminder of the aristocracy so vilified by Smith. Whereas Percy, despite subtitling his work *Recollections of a Planter's Son*, never quite comes to terms with his father's looming presence, Smith applauds her parents as rebels. Consider her dedication: "In memory of my Mother and Father who valiantly tried to keep their nine children in touch with wholeness even though reared in a segregated culture" (n.p.). By stressing their focus on wholeness, Smith implies that southerners who are fixated on the necessity of segregation lead inherently fractured lives, caught up in the anxiety that results from obsessing over racial purity. In her foreword to the 1961 revised edition, she claims that she wrote the memoir "because I had to find out what life in a segregated culture had done to me, one person; I had to put down on paper these experiences so that I could see their meaning for me" (13). In spite of this description, *Killers of the Dream* is an unconventional memoir, far less focused on the particularities of Smith's life than Percy's, a fact she acknowledges when stating, "I realize this is personal memoir, in one sense; in another sense, it is Every Southerner's memoir" (21). Scott Romine comments on this aspect of Smith's work, noting that one of her strategies is in "constructing oneself as a Southern outsider, one who has impeccable credentials as a Southerner but who has eluded Southern constraints on verbal expression," ultimately rendering herself as a "Southern Everywoman" ("Framing Southern Rhetoric" 96). Later, Smith will state, "I shall not tell, here, of experiences that were different and special and belonged only to me, but those most white southerners born at the turn of the century share with each other" (27).

Rather than discuss the specifics of her life as Percy does, Smith designs her memoir to showcase how ideologies are passed on to the younger generation, both in how racism is taught and in a distinct prejudicial attitude toward the poor. On southern defensiveness, she explains that "the breathing symbols we made of the blackness and the whiteness . . . the metaphors we created and watched ourselves turning into" morphed into the "shaky myths we leaned on even as we changed them into weapons to defend us against external events" (12). And while Smith does not include specific descriptions of racial violence in the manner that various fiction writers have, she does discuss the ways in which such events became magnified in children's minds: "Now, suddenly, shoving out pleasures and games and stinging questions come the TERRORS: the Ku Klux Klan and the lynchings I did not see but recreated from whispers of grownups . . . the gentle back-door cruelties of 'nice people' which scared me more than the cross burnings . . . and the singsong voices of politicians who preached their demonic suggestions to us as if elected by Satan to do so" (12).

Killers of the Dream is noted for Smith's attention to the relationship between racism and sexism and subverts the realm of white masculine privilege that dominates Percy's text. Near the outset of *Killers*, Smith observes that "neither the Negro nor sex was often discussed at length in our home," adding later that she had learned "a terrifying disaster would befall the South if ever I treated a Negro as my social equal and as terrifying a disaster would befall my family if ever I were to have a baby outside of marriage" (27–28). She also discusses how patriarchal regulation started basically from infancy. In part 2 (fittingly titled "The White Man's Burden"), in a chapter titled "The Lessons," she explains, "By the time we were five years old we had learned, without hearing the words, that masturbation is wrong and segregation is right, and each had become a dread taboo that must never be broken, for we believed God, whom we feared and tried desperately to love, had made the rules concerning not only Him and our parents, but our bodies and Negroes" (83–84).

In her prolonged discussion of the "three ghost stories" that haunt the modern South, Smith outlines an overt response to Percy's paternalism and the type of commentary that bemoans aristocratic whites' somehow being "owned" by, or otherwise being the victims of, blacks. Smith structures the stories by painting the South not as the nostalgic and unblemished world so recalled by the nostalgists but as a ghostly, spectral, and foreboding land. She writes, "And everywhere there were the ghosts wandering restlessly through our everyday lives. Stories about haunted houses on the edge of town—what southerner does not remember!—merely took our minds off our own haunted lives and gave us reasons for our fears. We gratefully accepted the ghosts because they gave names of our fears and we urged the grown-ups to tell us again and again about them" (112). Rather than Percy's apparent determination to either ignore or wish away the reality of southern hypocrisy and the lingering damage of racism and paternalism, Smith works to strip away their power: "These ghost relationships still haunt the Southern mind to such an extent that many of today's most urgent problems cannot be dealt with rationally. . . . They are ghosts that must be laid. Perhaps the only way to do it is to uncover them and see for ourselves the dusty nothingness beneath their masks" (116). The three relationships—"white man and colored woman, white father and colored children, white child and his beloved colored nurse"—are portrayed as fundamentally damaging to all southern children, and especially those women who find themselves "pushed away on that lonely pedestal called Sacred Womanhood" (134, 137).

Throughout the chapter on the ghost stories, Smith adeptly relates them to the criminality and barbarity of the Ku Klux Klan and the often-tacit support the Klan received from other whites. She notes that this attitude about sex and race led to a realm of "mass hysteria," colored by their "terrifying complex of guilt, anxiety, sex jealousy, and loneliness," which resulted in institutions such as the Klan, which could fuse such ideas into communal celebrations of whiteness (122). The Klan could serve, then, as a corrective to male anxiety by letting its members destroy blacks who threaten the realm of white female purity, which, again, was molded and concocted by sexually anxious whites. In stark contrast, Percy presents the Klan as both helpful in the past and largely inconsequential in the present:

> We had read in the newspapers that over in Atlanta some fraud was claiming to have revived the old Ku Klux Klan which during recon-struction days had played so desperate but on the whole so helpful a part in keeping the peace and preventing mob violence. This Atlanta monstrosity was not even a bastard of the old organization which General Forrest had headed and disbanded. This thing obviously was a money-making scheme without ideals or ideas. (231–32)

Smith, however, rightly notes that the contemporaneous Klan had far more impact on the southern psyche, based in hatred of blacks, paternalistic "'protecting' of womanhood," and disgust for "unions" and "middle-class 'deviationists'" (123).

The Klan (and the South at large, to an extent) used this widespread ideology to further the impact of its conservative mind-set, perhaps none so obvious as lynch law. Smith writes, "The lynched Negro becomes not an object that must die but a receptacle for every man's dammed-up hate, and a receptacle for every man's forbidden feelings," a devastating and chilling note on the ritualistic and unbridled violence so frequently categorized by black authors, as in James Baldwin's story "Going to Meet the Man" (162). Smith also notes the ways in which lynch law was formulated not at the request of the victimized women but rather by those men wishing to maintain their patriarchal hold on power; thus *Killers* works to dispel the widespread myths placed on women by men. For example, she describes the formation of the Association of Southern Women for the Prevention of Lynching in 1930, noting that the women set out to "commit treason against a southern tradition set up by men" as a response to white male dominance and hypocrisy, particularly sexual hypocrisy (144). Smith lambasts men who had "whipped up lynchings, organized Klans, burned crosses, aroused the poor and ignorant to wild excitement by an obscene, perverse imagery describing the 'menace' of Negro men hiding behind every cypress waiting to rape 'our' women," all in the name of defending "*sacred womanhood*," "*purity*," and "*preserving the home*" (145). After correctly identifying these loci of anxiety, Smith takes matters a step further by proclaiming that women do not, in fact, need protection: "They said calmly that they were not afraid of being raped; as for their sacredness, they could take care of it themselves; they did not need the chivalry of a lynching to protect them and did not want it" (145). Such an attitude would, of course, be antithetical to the core of southern white male identity, and indeed, Percy seldom gives any prolonged attention in his work to women; without relying on the flimsy rhetoric regarding rapacious black sexuality, white men would have to face the truth of their brutal treatment of blacks. The idea of outspoken women, too, was a signal of possible anxiety, as

Smith writes, "No one, of thousands of white men, had any notion how much or how little each woman knew about his private goings-on. Some who had never been guilty in act began to equate adolescent fantasies with reality, and there was confusion everywhere" (145–46). And toward the end of the "Three Ghost Stories" section, Smith offers a culminating statement about the linkage between patriarchy and white supremacy; she observes that white attitudes had been shaped by "high interest at the bank and low wages in the mills and gullied fields and lynchings and Ku Klux Klan and segregation and sacred womanhood and revivals, and Prohibition," with a final note that "no part of this memory can be understood without recalling all of it," an early intersectional response to the South's pervasive issues (136). Ultimately, then, these ghost stories are examples Smith uses to respond to the idea that paternalism and moderate white response to issues like segregation so championed by Percy do little to quell the tensions in the South and in fact further inflame the passions of whites dedicated to upholding the supremacy they regarded as under threat since Reconstruction.

As is the case with *Killers*, Percy's memoir is perhaps most noted for its treatment of race, but a consideration of both authors' treatment of class serves to extend our knowledge of the intersectional relationship between class and racism, as well as to shed more light on an underconsidered component of Smith's career. Throughout *Lanterns*, Percy takes strides toward establishing his ongoing paternalist approach to race relations. This hierarchy also extends to poor whites throughout, and the language Percy metes out against them is, surprisingly, harsher at times than during his discussion of blacks. Ultimately, if blacks exist in *Lanterns* as the cause of lingering anxiety and patronizing condescension for Percy and the aristocratic class he represents, poor whites stand as oppressive interlopers, Snopesian intruders into his revered Delta country. From their first mention, poor whites are demarcated as subhuman and inherently inferior to Percy and his ilk: "Another element leaving almost as little impress, though still extant, is the 'river-rat.' He is white, Anglo-Saxon, with twists of speech and grammatical forms current in Queen Anne's day or earlier, and a harsh 'r' strange to all Southerners except mountaineers. Where he comes from no one knows or cares" (16). That the poor whites, the "river-rats," are described as almost forgettable locates them as existing near the bottom rung of the social hierarchy. Percy claims that nobody cares where they come from, though he does briefly claim that "some find in [the river-rat] the descendant of those pirates who used to infest the river as far up as Memphis. It seems more likely his forefathers were out-of-door, ne'er-do-well nomads of the pioneer days," though their presence, particularly in Percy's later description of his father's political career, is clearly a site of contention for the author (16–17). His physical description of these poor whites is similarly critical and insulting: "Illiterate, suspicious, intensely clannish, blond, and usually ugly, river-rats make ideal bootleggers. . . . They lead a life apart, uncouth, unclean, lawless, vaguely alluring. Their contact with the land world around them consists largely in being hauled into court, generally for murder. No Negro is ever a river-rat" (17). The "usually ugly" remark is significant in that it again creates a hierarchy of whiteness where, despite his Anglo-Saxon origins (as a contrast, Percy discusses his own family's French origins more favorably), the "river-rat" is markedly inferior to Percy's family. The "murder" comment paints poor whites as impulsive and rash, prone to making their presence in society too open and too visible. Later Percy describes the "three dissimilar threads" that compose the "basic fiber" of the Delta as "the old slave-holders," "the poor whites, who owned no slaves, whose manual labor lost its dignity from being in competition with slave labor," and "the Negroes" (19).

But while this trajectory seems clearly to place poor whites between Percy's class and blacks, the truth is more vexed, as Percy frequently defines these whites in relation to blacks. Of blacks, Percy makes an early comment akin to a patient parent scolding rascally children: "Just now we are happy that the brother in black is still the tiller of our soil, the hewer of our wood, our servants, troubadours, and criminals. His manners offset his inefficiency, his vices have the charm of amiable weaknesses, he is a pain and a grief to live with, a solace and a delight" (21). Part of what makes blacks tolerable—here as elsewhere in the memoir—is Percy's hope that they as a group "know their place" and perform functions considered too menial for his class. The aristocracy is defined through their relationship to the labor that props them up and maintains their position, from the historical plantations to the remnants of that culture, such as the continued employment of black mammies, caretakers, and servants. Blacks induce anxiety when they begin to seek a path upward and beyond these strict social paradigms, as when they desire camaraderie or jest in a manner that assumes too much familiarity. But poor whites cause consternation because their own place in society is more difficult to pin down; they should not, Percy seems to suggest, occupy the same labor sphere as blacks, yet their upward mobility and urge to distinguish themselves from their perceived inferiors trouble him. He writes: "Intellectually and spiritually they are inferior to the Negro, whom they hate. Suspecting secretly they are inferior to him, they must do something to him to prove to themselves their superiority. At their door must be laid the disgraceful riots and lynchings gloated over and exaggerated by Negrophiles the world over" (20). In addition to the highly troubling remark that attention to lynchings has been "exaggerated," Percy's entire statement here is ironic; he observes that poor whites face anxiety in regard to blacks, without recognizing that his text serves as testament that upper-class whites face anxiety in response to both poor whites and blacks. Percy's language here is suspiciously vague; he fails to describe in what manner these whites would feel inferior to blacks, instead attempting to lump them together as a homogeneous class with a single, shared mind-set. By precluding the possibility of individuality, Percy shifts blame for lynchings and other racial violence onto the lower class, ignoring the fact that well-to-do whites share culpability, either by participating themselves or by fostering a culture in which lynch mobs could operate without fear of reprisal.

One concrete example from Percy's life will serve as a precursor to Smith's attempts at sympathy and an engagement with the

Rewriting the South in *Killers of the Dream*   59

South's social hierarchies, as opposed to Percy, who offers blanket statements such as "I can forgive them as the Lord God forgives, but admire them, trust them, love them—never" (20). Scott Romine notes that Percy attempts to "rationalize the social order," and while "much of his narrative concerns the poor white, the nature of this group provides little resistance to Percy's worldview" (*Narrative* 115). Nowhere is this clearer than in Percy's ire toward what he regards as poor whites encroaching on the South's political sphere in a story about his father's political career. After the death of Senator Anselm McLaurin in 1909, the Mississippi legislature opted to fill the empty seat, which, at the time, was favored to go to the race-baiting demagogue James K. Vardaman, known as the "Great White Chief." As Percy describes Vardaman, he was "a kindly, vain demagogue unable to think, and given to emotions he considered noble," a man whose speaking skills resembled "bastard emotionalism and raven-tressed rant," and whose political ideology was no more complex than the fact that he "stood for the poor white against the 'nigger'—those were his qualifications as a statesman" (143–44). This extended description is used to emphasize differences between Vardaman and Percy's father, LeRoy, whom he regards as an incisive, fair man; though LeRoy at first viewed Vardaman as a "splendid ham actor" and merely a "mischievous" race-baiter, Percy presents him as unable to abide the idea of such a demagogue in office (144).

In contrast, LeRoy is described as an idealistic alternative: "Father wanted to be a force for good government, but he did not want to hold office. He did not want to be senator from Mississippi, but he wanted to keep Vardaman from being. Vardaman stood for all he considered vulgar and dangerous" (144). After detailing how his father was chosen as the strongest anti-Vardaman candidate, Percy turns to the frenzy surrounding the election to make more pointed critiques of lower-class whites; whereas his father's "integrity, courage, and intelligence" mattered in a past "world of honor," Percy describes a new world, the "golden age of demagoguery, the age of rabble-rousers and fire-eaters," granted life by the kinds of people who would vote for the likes of Vardaman and later Bilbo (148). Such people are described as sordid and barbaric; Percy recalls a campaign stop where the crowd gathered with hampers of eggs ready to toss at LeRoy:

> I looked over the ill-dressed, surly audience, unintelligent and slinking, and heard him appeal to them for fair treatment of the Negro and explain to them the tariff and the Panama tolls situation. I studied them as they milled about. They were the sort of people that lynch Negroes, that mistake hoodlumism for wit, and cunning for intelligence, that attend revivals and fight and fornicate in the bushes afterwards. They were undiluted Anglo-Saxons. They were the sovereign voter. It was so horrible it seemed unreal. (149)

Percy portrays himself and his father here as outsiders, looking down on their inferiors and telling—not showing—them what is best for their lives. Percy also reveals physical anxiety; he is openly repelled by the vibrant lustiness of the crowd, their fighting and fornicating, and his awareness of their physicality stands in contrast to his own stationary, reserved role as spectator. In another instance, the crowd is portrayed as uncivilized, whooping and yelling until the "din was insane and intolerable. . . . Obviously the crowd was determined to make it impossible for him to speak at all" (150). Throughout *Lanterns*, Percy makes clear that part of the masculine code—which is obviously white, since blacks are so often referred to as burdensome—of the Delta is the importance of restraint and control; the "obscene pandemonium" of the crowd flies in the face of said code and marks the start of a new era where the gentility has been replaced by inferior stock. After LeRoy loses the election, the family opts for a vacation to Greece, a site far removed from this New South, where father and son can mutually reconnect to a noblesse oblige that has long colored their views on race and class.

For Smith, the connection between aristocratic or upper-class whites and poor southerners stems from her thesis that poor whites are frequently victimized by demagogues who "fatten on the poor

Rewriting the South in *Killers of the Dream* 61

man's vote" by preaching what the poor wish to hear, namely, that they are superior to the blacks whom they hate and whom the wealthy whites are afraid of, lest the groups unite out of class solidarity (121). At the beginning of the "Giants in the Earth" section of *Killers*, Smith attempts to push back against the likes of elite, yet often geographically distant, commentators like Percy, noting, "Only a man or woman who has traveled in childhood the old sand or clay roads of the South in buggy or wagon, who has stayed in the country after nightfall, can know what distance and darkness meant in the making of the rural mind of the South" (159). In Smith's reckoning, the relationship between rich and poor is predatory, though not in the manner seen in Percy's reckoning; instead, poor whites are manipulated and have their base impulses fed to serve the political and economic benefit of their supposed superiors: "Southern culture has put few words in the mind to make the difference between human and animal. The words in the white mind are words that turn the Negro into animal, words deliberately fed to people to place the Negro beneath the level of human, to make him not only animal but a 'menace'" (161). Though the emphasis on whites being "deliberately fed" this knowledge is not necessarily a novel observation from Smith, her extended discussion seeks to note that the poor have been inculcated with such behaviors and beliefs as a means of suppression.

In noting the "terrifying ignorance" that pervades the rural South, Smith might seem to adhere to the same tropes noted by Percy. But unlike Percy, who simply vilifies and blames the poor for their conditions, Smith seeks to elicit sympathy and understanding. She asks rhetorically, "What good does it do to repeat illiteracy figures to readers whose minds have been nourished well since they were born? How can we who were fed so bountifully feel what it means to live with a mind emptied of words, bereft of ideas and facts, unknowing of books and man-made beauty?" (163). Smith goes on to argue for what amounts to borderline separatism: "It would have been far better for them had they been ignored, as were most of the peasants of the world until communism's recent efforts," but politicians "needed the rural people and used them as ruthlessly as Negroes were used when they were needed" (164). This argument further accentuates and details the idea of hierarchization that so often colors the treatment of poor whites, particularly when it came to establishing the "worth" of white skin: Smith notes white skin as "the poor white's most precious possession, a 'charm' staving off utter dissolution" that allowed one to "forget that you were eaten up with malaria and hookworm" and "lived in a shanty and ate pot-likker and corn bread, and worked long hours for nothing. Nobody could take away from you this whiteness that made you and your way of life 'superior'" (164–65). Smith's commentary lends to another sweeping assessment of the history of poor whites, noting that "those on the other side of the chasm from the large slave owner—and that was most of the South—came to be called 'poor whites' and 'crackers,' 'red necks,' 'hill billies,' and 'peckerwoods,' and a startling lack of sympathy for them slipped into [the] speech and writings and hearts of the planter class," who ultimately "denied Tobacco Road" and "wrote off the man who lived on Tobacco Road as a liability to democracy for it is his vote that keeps the demagogue in power. Now, today, they fear him because they helped make him what he was" (171). In her essay "Buying a New World with Confederate Bills," Smith further explains how the poor white, "torn by feelings of inferiority," feels compelled to "assert his superiority to the Negro and his identification with the 'gentleman'" (22). And unlike so many others, Smith offers a personal account voicing her own sympathy for the poor: "Having lived my early life in a Deep South town and much of my recent life in the mountains, I have a bond with rural people which I cherish. The stereotypes built of them by those who are trying to manipulate them are partly true, of course; but partly false. They do have little learning and can be stubborn as mules; but they have conscience," adding that she fears them less than the "demagogic leaders who shoulder the people intimately but exploit them ruthlessly" (174).

The divide between the rich and poor white is discussed at length in *Killers* in a chapter titled "Two Men and a Bargain," which tells a

Rewriting the South in *Killers of the Dream* 63

metaphoric tale of "Mr. Rich White" and "Mr. Poor White" and the agreement between the pair. As Mr. Rich White explains it, "There're two jobs down here that need doing: Somebody's got to tend to the living, and somebody's got to tend to the nigger. . . . You boss the nigger, and I'll boss the money" (176). Even more obvious rhetoric comes into play when Mr. Rich White expands on his rationale for the class divide: "If you ever get restless when you don't have a job or your roof leaks, or the children look puny and shoulder blades stick out more than natural, all you need do is remember you're a sight better than the black man" (177). Smith makes clear that even without specific examples, the racial situation in the South can be identified and explained as being precipitated by anxiety; Mr. Rich White has an imperative need to maintain a divide between poor whites and blacks lest their position be threatened: "It never occurred to Mr. Poor White that with a bargain the Negro could help him raise wages" (179). The simplicity of the metaphor (one also used by W. J. Cash in *The Mind of the South*) reveals that while racist treatment of blacks was based on a myriad of reasons, at its core, it was nearly always predicated in some form on the dual concerns of hierarchical wealth and racial anxiety, prompting whites to seek to maintain segregation so as to maintain their economic dominance or, in the case of poorer whites, to hold on to notions of honor built on a belief in natal white superiority. Smith also uses the metaphor in *Our Faces, Our Words* as she pens a fictionalized monologue of a young white woman despondent at her father's bigotry: "You went to Harvard—and yet you fall for the lies Mr. Rich White told Mr. Poor White long ago, to keep him satisfied with poverty and sharecropping" (287). And again in "Buying a New World with Confederate Bills," Smith describes how poor white men are led to believe they are "as good as" wealthier whites only because they added the coda "For look at all the black folks we both are better than!" (21). Thus, in various instances, Smith, along with other writers who presented women as indignant at the patronizing treatment they received, help bring to light this widespread pathology of southern anxiety and its relationship to race.

Unsurprisingly, Smith was nervous about the potential reception of her book, even in the closing chapters of *Killers*. In the revised edition, she reflects, "I use the word *we* on many pages of this book: yet, never in this movement backward or forward has there been unity in the South. There have always been thousands of dissenters whose voices are muffled, whose acts are ignored" (223). In setting out to write a corrective to the nostalgic sentiment that was so pervasive in writing about the South, Smith also set out to respond to the paternalism that she regarded as so damaging to women's lives; in a 1950 report, she cataloged a variety of responses to the work, noting wryly, "No—in answer to numerous queries—the Klan has not burned my home down. And people still 'speak to me' in Clayton" ("Report from Lillian Smith" 128). In response to the question "Do women like the book better than men?" she notes, "Yes, I think they do. But men like it also," though she also remarks that "a few men have exploded in wrath about these ghost stories" (130). And while *Killers* is perhaps so well remembered for its universality, she closes the report with the personal hope that despite the difficulty she faced in writing the book, she

> wanted, by laying bare my own childhood experiences, to help others understand this strange ceremonial we call "segregation": to see it not as racial segregation but as a profound withdrawal from life, a denial of reality. . . . I wanted my book to give insight, to stir imaginations, so that we can accept ourselves and all the earth's people as human beings, and once accepting, can go on with the job of making our new world—a world of open spaces with no walls in minds or between nations to throw their shadows across our children's lives. That was my dream. (131–32)

Though the South and the country writ large may have defeated de jure segregation after the *Brown* ruling and passage of the Civil Rights Act, Smith's words ring as true in the first quarter of the twenty-first century as they did during the most fevered debates of the midcentury. Smith's example of resistance, then, will hopefully continue to serve as a model; not a comfortable or an easy one, but a resilient and determined arbiter of will and courage in the face of public opprobrium.

Notes

A version of this chapter originally appeared in Justin Mellette, *Peculiar Whiteness: Racial Anxiety and Poor Whites in Southern Literature, 1900–1965* (Jackson: University Press of Mississippi, 2021).

1. In Denis Brogan's introduction to the 1971 British edition, he observes that among the work's weaknesses is "the almost complete neglect of the Negroes. 'The South' is the white South" (n.p.).

Works Cited

Andrews, William L. "In Search of a Common Identity: The Self and the South in Four Mississippi Autobiographies." *Southern Review*, vol. 24, no. 1, 1988, pp. 47–62.

Baldwin, James. *Going to Meet the Man*. Dial, 1965.

Brogan, Denis. Introduction. *The Mind of the South*, by W. J. Cash, Thames and Hudson, 1971, n.p.

Cash, W. J. *The Mind of the South*. Thames and Hudson, 1971.

Gladney, Margaret Rose, ed. *How Am I to Be Heard? Letters of Lillian Smith*. U of North Carolina P, 1993.

Gladney, Margaret Rose. Preface. Gladney, xiii–xviii.

Griggs, Sutton. *The Hindered Hand*. Orion, 1905.

Hobson, Fred. *Tell about the South: The Southern Rage to Explain*. Louisiana State UP, 1983.

Percy, William Alexander. *Lanterns on the Levee*. Alfred A. Knopf, 1941.

Romine, Scott. "Framing Southern Rhetoric: Lillian Smith's Narrative Persona in *Killers of the Dream*," *South Atlantic Review*, vol. 59, no. 2, 1994, pp. 95–111.

Romine, Scott. *The Narrative Forms of Southern Community*. Louisiana State UP, 1999.

Smith, Lillian. "Buying a New World with Confederate Bills." *South Today*, vol. 7, no. 2, Winter 1942–43, pp. 7–30.

Smith, Lillian. "Dope with Lime." *North Georgia Review*, vol. 16, 1941, pp. 4–6.

Smith, Lillian. *Killers of the Dream*. W. W. Norton, 1994.

Smith, Lillian. Letter to George Brockway, July 3, 1965. Gladney, 322–23.

Smith, Lillian. Letter to George Reynolds, February 14, 1940. Gladney, 35–41.

Smith, Lillian. Letter to the *New York Times*, April 4, 1948. Gladney, 119–22.

Smith, Lillian. *Our Faces, Our Words: A Lillian Smith Reader*, edited by Margaret Rose Gladney and Lisa Hodgens, U of Georgia P, 2016.

Smith, Lillian. "Report from Lillian Smith on *Killers of the Dream*, February 18, 1950." Gladney, pp. 128–32.

Wise, Benjamin E. *William Alexander Percy: The Curious Life of a Mississippi Planter and Sexual Freethinker*. U of North Carolina P, 2012.

Wyatt-Brown, Bertram. "Will Percy and *Lanterns on the Levee* Revisited." *Storytelling, History, and the Postmodern South*, edited by Jason Phillips, Louisiana State UP, 2013, pp. 12–42.

CHAPTER 3

"The Intricate Weavings of Unnumbered Threads": Personal and Societal Trauma in Lillian Smith's *Killers of the Dream*

—Emily Pierce Cummins

In her "A Southerner Talking" column for the *Chicago Defender* on November 27, 1948, Lillian Smith writes that in rereading *The Masters and the Slaves*, Gilberto Freyre's wide-ranging study of the formation of Brazilian society first published in English in 1946, she had realized that "in many ways it is a better book on the strange relationships between races and cultures" (147) than the Swedish sociologist Gunnar Myrdal's *An American Dilemma*. Myrdal's classic work on racial segregation and discrimination, published in 1944, had identified the source of the "Negro problem" in the conflict between the American Creed—the set of values fundamental to the self-image of white Americans, including a commitment to "liberty, equality, justice, and fair opportunity for everybody" (xlviii)—and the reality of social and economic conditions of African Americans. In the book, Myrdal posits that the typical white American was "actually also a good Christian and honestly devoted to the ideals of human brotherhood and the Golden Rule" (xlviii) but did not understand how these ideals remained inaccessible to African Americans, primarily because of widespread racial discrimination and attitudes toward African Americans' ability to achieve them. As

Myrdal argues, the "Negro problem" was in fact a "white problem": the solution to the dilemma of racial inequality in America was for white Americans to live up to their own values of fairness, justice, and economic opportunity for everyone.

While Smith expresses "great respect and admiration" for Myrdal and his "fine, scholarly" work, she implies that his emphasis on abstract idealism and economic statistics is somewhat limiting, preferring Freyre's refusal "to consider segregation and its evils and the white man and his economics out of context with the whole of the life of the people" (147). In *The Masters and the Slaves*, Smith writes, Freyre examines "religion, ideals about death and birth, child care, food habits, even food recipes" (147) and demonstrates "his awareness of the profound effect which attitudes toward sex and body have on a people's attitudes not only toward so-called 'inferior' people but toward themselves and money and death and the creative process" (147). Although Myrdal's economic analysis is valuable in its own way, Smith clearly favors Freyre's intimate "inside" perspective on Brazilian culture, with its emphasis on the interconnectedness of all aspects of society to explain complex social problems.

The most important limitation of Myrdal's work, according to Smith, is that "he had not lived his way through the dilemma and that he was here for so short a time" (147). Unlike Freyre, a native of Brazil, Myrdal was an outsider to the culture he analyzed, and while his objectivity in *An American Dilemma* might be perceived as a strength, Smith argues that the most effective critique can only come from the inside and derive from deep personal knowledge that results from having been born and raised in a particular culture. She writes:

> I do not believe it is possible to understand the white man in America and his strange paranoid notions about his superiority without considering his equally strange childhood and the training he received before he was six years old, the heavy guilt laid on heart and body while both were so young and weak, and finally the strange fruit which this kind of training has borne, not only of White Supremacy

Personal and Societal Trauma in *Killers of the Dream*   69

but of mental illness, alcoholism, child delinquency, exploitation and war-making. That was what I tried to say in my novel published five years ago. The "strange fruit" I wrote of was not lynching or miscegenation (a word I hate) but the white man himself and his children and his Tobacco Roads and his own wasted life: the "strange fruit" was man dehumanized by a *culture that is not good for the growth of either white or colored children.* (147–48; italics in original)

Smith emphasizes that southern culture must be taken as a whole, that segregation, sin, guilt, religion, and social dysfunction are threads in a dense weave, and to pull on one thread is to unravel an entire network of associations. Children—both black and white—raised in such an environment internalize the culture and are, on some level, suffocated by its tightly woven fabric, growing into the strange fruit produced by damaged seeds and restricted limbs. Although Myrdal argues that equal access to education is key to overcoming racial inequality, Smith recognizes that education is merely one more thread that cannot be separated from the cultural whole. She writes, "One of the tragic elements in the American dilemma seems to me to be the eagerness with which members of the Negro race take on the sins of the white race in the name of 'education'" (148). For Myrdal, the American dilemma is that whites do not live up to the values they claim to believe in; for Smith, the dilemma of the South is that southerners do. Smith's attempt to explain this situation from an insider's perspective in all its complexity is the origin of *Killers of the Dream.*

In a 1940 letter to George Reynolds, director of fellowships for the Julius Rosenwald Fund, requesting research funding for a book on southern literature and culture, Smith writes, "Contemporary southern literature itself cannot be understood and appraised out of its societal-racial-psychological context" (39). In Smith's eyes, only a southerner who has experienced firsthand the traumas of the South's history and society could write a book like *Killers of the Dream.* In the proposal, Smith writes that her book will "gather up the economic, cultural, political, psychological strands that tie the South into its present hard knot" (40). Though this particular book proposal never came to fruition, Margaret Rose Gladney notes that it "contains the seeds of major themes Smith later developed in *Killers*," specifically the importance of these tangled strands to her analysis (39).

This study investigates Smith's powerful use of the thread/fabric and ghost metaphors to develop the reader's understanding of southern trauma. Smith, an upper-class white southerner, was viewed by many as a traitor for her civil rights writing and activism, yet by using these metaphors, she effectively guides readers through the complicated factors of southern identity and argues convincingly that healing requires us to process historical and societal trauma, a process as important for whites as for blacks.

Trauma is central to Smith's analysis, not only how trauma is experienced and processed on the individual level, but also the cyclical and intergenerational nature of large-scale and historical trauma. Smith processes her own trauma in the retelling of her childhood and simultaneously unfolds the larger context of the region's childhood trauma. By breaking down the societal norms and taboos of the South in her personal story, Smith demonstrates how the trauma of slavery and Jim Crow repeats itself across generations for everyone affected by it, white and black, creating an intergenerational psychological wound that is perpetuated by cultural and societal forces for the sake of "saving face." Michelle Balaev, in her introduction to *Contemporary Approaches in Literary Trauma Theory*, states that "the evolution of trauma theory in literary criticism might best be understood in terms of the changing psychological definitions of trauma as well as the semiotic, rhetorical, and social concerns that are part of the study of trauma in literature and society" (2). She goes on to say that "this shift in literary trauma theory has produced a set of critical practices that place more focus on the particular social components and cultural contexts of traumatic experience" ("Literary Trauma Theory Reconsidered" 3). Literary trauma theory as it applies on both a personal and societal scale is fitting for exploring Smith's work, as it considers the multifaceted impact of social and historical trauma.[1] In the case of the South, many events created its large-scale societal and historical traumas, co-occurring with personal and intergenerational traumas, especially with regard to race. Through her use of thread and ghost metaphors, Smith unveils these traumas to release their hold on southern minds and culture.

To emphasize the interconnection of the semiotic, rhetorical, and social, Smith frequently uses imagery of woven threads when describing how sin, sex, and segregation interact with trauma and memory. In *Killers*, she presents the idea as such: "Out of the intricate weavings of unnumbered threads, I shall pick out a few strands, a few designs that have to do with what we call color and race . . . and politics . . . and money and how it is made . . . and religion . . . and sex and the body image . . . and love . . . and the dreams of the Good and the killers of dreams" (27).

This passage is, in a sense, her abstract, outlining what Jay Watson calls "the dense weave of 'sin, sex, and segregation' . . . [that] Smith locates at the heart of Southern social relations during the early decades of [that] century" (472). McKay Jenkins also references this image, writing, "To pull apart these threads, Smith throughout her work explored the psychological damage, the 'splitting,' that is done when racist discourse overpowers compassion or empathy or tenderness" (102). The threads begin their weave around each life from birth, creating traumas that tangle with those of others within the southern tapestry.

Throughout the chapter titled "The Lessons," Smith details what southerners learn as children about sin, sex, and segregation. Smith describes the effects of these threads as a frame, stating that "the warped, distorted frame we have put around every Negro child from birth is around every white child also. Each is on a different side of the frame, but each is pinioned there" (39). Ideology creates trauma that molds children as they grow, and even the best of intentions as an adult cannot change that: "We are stunted and warped and in our lifetime cannot grow straight again any more than can a tree, put in a steel-like twisting frame when young, grow tall and straight when the frame is torn away at maturity" (Smith, *Killers* 39). Thus the trauma is maintained in the greater society and passed on to the next generation, creating a cycle that perpetuates the large-scale trauma from generation to generation as the societal traumas are impressed on each individual from birth. Speaking about what children like her were taught about sex, Smith explains, "By the time we were five years old we had learned, without hearing the words, that masturbation is wrong, and segregation is right, and each had become a dread taboo that must never be broken, for we believed God . . . had made the rules" (83–84). The lessons were simple: "We were told that [God] loved us, and then we were told that He would burn us in everlasting flames of hell if we displeased him" (85). She elaborates on the guilt associated with sexuality in particular but notes the redemption granted by the simple virtue of being white: "Though your body is a thing of shame and mystery, and curiosity about it is not good . . . your white skin proves that you are better than all other people on this earth. . . . The lesson on segregation was only a logical extension of the lessons on sex and white supremacy and God" (89–90). The threads of race, sex, and social status interlace, creating a cultural fabric that covers southern children from birth, swaddling them in the anxieties and traumas of their society and history. This becomes normalized as the cycle is repeated through generations, the weave of sin, sex, and segregation tightening as they settle into the subconscious. These threads and the cultural fabric are upheld by southern tradition and are seen as the normal way of life, further perpetuating the cycle of trauma.

Personal traumas, created and maintained by historical and societal traumas, influence each new generation. Parents tell their children, "This is how it's done here," a belief that is confirmed by the societal traumas that shaped their own lives. Despite internal turmoil sparked by such beliefs, they are perpetuated by the momentum of history and social custom, which creates intergenerational trauma. Balaev writes in "Trends in Literary Trauma Theory" that "a massive trauma experienced by a group in the historical past can be experienced by an individual living centuries later who shares a similar attribute of the historical group, such as sharing the same race, religion, nationality, or gender due to the timeless, repetitious, and infectious characteristics of traumatic experience and memory" (152). Balaev's description would clearly apply to African Americans oppressed by slavery and Jim Crow, but what gives Smith's argument its power is her insistence that the interwoven threads of sin, sex, and segregation entangle white people as much as black.

To bring this tangle into the light where even whites can see it, Smith equates her childhood to that of every other white child in the South. In her report on *Killers*, "in reply to hundreds of letters which cannot be individually answered now," she writes, "The book is not only my biography as a southerner; it is theirs also. I think that many know in their hearts that to read it will be like turning the yellowed leaves of their own diary" (*How Am I to Be Heard?* 128–29). Smith repeats the sentiment in the foreword of the revised edition of *Killers*, stating, "I realize this is personal memoir, in one sense; in another sense, it is Every Southerner's memoir" (21). Balaev argues, "A single conceptualization of trauma will likely never fit the multiple and often contradictory depictions of trauma in literature because texts cultivate a wide variety of values that reveal individual and cultural understandings of the self, memory, and society" ("Literary Trauma Theory Reconsidered" 8). However, Smith builds a strong case that her reader has lived the same traumas that she has.

In writing *Killers*, Smith processes her own experience of growing up choked by the interwoven threads of sin, sex, and segregation, inviting the reader to face the trauma with her. In the foreword to the revised edition, she offers testimony of the healing effects: "I am different. Because I wrote it. In the writing I explored layers of my natures which I had never touched before; in reliving my distant small childhood my imagination stretched and enclosed my whole life; my beliefs changed as I wrote them down" (14). *Killers* itself reflects how one processes trauma by untangling its threads, warning that until doing so, one will remain deformed. Balaev argues, "Trauma is only known through repetitive flashbacks that literally re-enact the event because the mind cannot represent it otherwise.... Traumatic experience is understood as a fixed and timeless photographic negative stored in an unlocatable place of the brain, but it maintains the ability to interrupt consciousness" ("Trends" 151). Throughout *Killers*, Smith interjects anecdotes from her life. These interjections feel organic, allowing the reader to process Smith's trauma as she does. For example, the story of the "little white girl" who came to stay with Smith's family temporarily—until it was discovered that the girl was not "white" at all and she was quickly returned to Colored Town—serves as a doorway through which the reader can peer at his or her own experience of the trauma caused by parental hypocrisy. In Smith's anecdote, the reader recognizes the pain of discovering that one's parents are not as pure and good as children tend to presume: "Something was wrong.... And I was shamed by their failure and frightened, for I felt they were no longer as powerful as I had thought. There was something Out There that was stronger than they and I could not bear to believe it" (37).

The recursive nature of the book itself reflects the processing of trauma. With each iteration of "sin, sex, and segregation," as well as her other themes, the tapestry depicting the South's trauma becomes clearer. For instance, Smith mentions her black nurse briefly in the first chapter of *Killers* but returns to give more details about her during the "Three Ghost Stories" chapter. Smith also references the white woman's pedestal several times before she explores the notion more fully in the chapter titled "The Women." Balaev illuminates the effect of this strategy: "Traumatic memory is rarely represented as an exact recalling of events. Rather, the construction of the past includes new details with each telling, or it is constructed from different perspectives, which demonstrates that memories of the traumatic experience are revised and actively rearranged according to the needs of the individual at a particular moment" ("Trends" 164). Smith seems to remember more details with each telling as she processes personal trauma as well as the large-scale societal and historical trauma that

Personal and Societal Trauma in *Killers of the Dream* 75

has affected her life. By revisiting memories again and again, she follows important threads, gradually revealing the sources of her troublesome behaviors, beliefs, and values.

Central to *Killers of the Dream* are stories about Laurel Falls, a girls' camp in Clayton, Georgia, which Smith ran for twenty-five years. Smith relays anecdotes about the camp to illustrate the potential of trauma processing. In the introduction to the 1994 edition of *Killers*, Margaret Rose Gladney writes:

> Through her work with the young women of Laurel Falls Camp, Smith found emotional access to her own childhood and awareness of the socialization process. . . . There also she came close to creating the world she wanted to live in, a world where every child could experience esteem, where individual creativity could be encouraged by a supportive community, where old ideas were questioned and new ones explored, and where differences could be appreciated. (2)

In the *Killers* chapter "The Stolen Future," Smith writes that "a procession of children had come to our mountain, stayed a few summers, passed on. Sensitive, intelligent, eager, quick with their questions, generous and honest—fine raw material for the future. And much of it has been wasted by a region that values color more than children" (75). Smith dedicates this chapter to describing the growth that occurred when the girls were encouraged to follow the threads of their values to their origins. She writes of the campers' creating their own version of *The Little Prince*, and the problems that arise when the Prince asks to play with all of the Earth's children. Chaos ensues; Smith reflects the campers' concerns: "'If he plays with children he must play with those in mill town and colored ones too, right here in Georgia.' 'Oh my goodness! Then we can't. And you know it. Why be so silly?' 'Down here we just can't—' 'Daddy says—' 'My mother says—'" (46). The campers' first response is to reject the Prince's request, citing the way things are done and what their parents have told them. The previous generation has influenced the next one, and the traumas, the threads of sin, sex, and segregation, are already wrapped around this new generation, as Smith's portrayal of the process of producing the drama shows.

In writing their play, the campers give the Prince the traveling companions of Conscience, Southern Tradition, Religion, and Science. Conscience is played as a nursemaid, Southern Tradition by eight dancers opening or closing paths for the Prince, and Religion and Science by several girls placed on two opposite balconies (Smith 44–45). After the chaos of the Prince's wanting to play with all of the Earth's children, Smith suggests that the Prince ask his traveling companions that represent southern ideology. Those playing the companions improvise based on what they know: Conscience refers to Southern Tradition on the issue of race, Southern Tradition does not listen to Religion or Science up on their balconies, and the Prince is not strong enough to fight Southern Tradition, not by himself, anyway (47–49). Smith finds a way to help the girls resolve their problem. The children change Religion to Love and say that in time, Love will come down from the balcony and help push Southern Tradition off the stage (50).

Smith marvels at the campers' ability to show the trauma the South perpetuates:

> It seems such a little thing, doesn't it? A few children gathered on a mountain making a play— . . . of Every Child living on a planet alone, who tries to reach out and embrace his universe and finds he cannot because Religion will not show him the way, and Science is too busy with the making of machines and gadgets and bombs to use its resources to help him, and Conscience has learned no new lessons since childhood, and only Southern Tradition is strong. (74)

The campers, despite, or perhaps because of, their age, have identified the major traumas within this tapestry created by sin, sex, and segregation, as well as how the cycle of trauma is maintained.

Although Smith's campers have shed light on the tightly woven fabric of segregation, she writes to urge the necessity of trauma

Personal and Societal Trauma in *Killers of the Dream*   77

processing on a larger scale. To that end, in addition to developing the thread metaphor, she employs the ghost to represent the South's projection of repressed guilt and fear. Smith describes the "haunted childhood [that] belongs to every southerner of [her] age," and uses the term "ghost stories" to elaborate on the relationships caused by societal trauma in the South. While discussing small southern towns, Smith writes, "And everywhere there were ghost stories wandering restlessly through our everyday lives. Stories about haunted houses on the edge of town—what southerner does not remember!—merely took our minds off our own haunted lives and gave us reasons for our fears" (112). Here she argues that the large-scale traumas that are the real cause of fear and anxiety remain unnamed as they haunt one throughout life. Smith also discusses the dangers of such projection in a speech about mobs, the Klan, and ghosts, given in 1961; she writes to her niece elaborating on this speech's message: "They [mobs and the Klan], too, let ghosts out, and turned living people into ghosts, into symbols. . . . The group listening to me got the point very quickly. I said all mobs let their ghosts out or transferred them or projected them on to living people—then they went on a ghost hunt" (letter to Marianne Fink, May 2, 1961, 274). The threads of sin, sex, and segregation are ignored, the blame placed on the subjects of ghost stories instead. This leads people to ignore that they are suffering trauma that splits the consciousness in such a way as to create further trauma. This dynamic is then maintained at the societal and historical level, creating a cycle of trauma.

Smith elaborates on this cycle through her discussion of the three ghost relationships of the South: "white man and colored woman, white father and colored children, white child and his beloved colored nurse—haunting the mind of the South and giving shape to our lives and souls" (134–35). Smith discusses what she calls the "back-yard temptation," the first ghost, where white male slave owners found the black women in the backyard more interesting than the white women in the front. Smith describes how southerners' denial of this sexual dynamic splits the consciousness traumatically:

> The more trails the white man made to back-yard cabins, the higher he raised his white wife on her pedestal when he returned to the big house. The higher the pedestal, the less he enjoyed her whom he had put there, for statues after all are only nice things to look at. . . . It was of course inevitable for him to suspect her of the sins he had committed so pleasantly and often. . . . In jealous panic [he] began to project his own sins on to the Negro male. (121)

Here Smith explains the stereotype of the oversexualized black male as a manifestation of white men's guilt. The black man, hence, became the southern bogeyman. The insidious threads weave tighter, inflicting and maintaining trauma that grows to the historical and societal level from the personal. False accusations against black men continue to be a common phenomenon today.

"The South's rejected children" are a result of these relationships (*Killers* 124). Smith elaborates, "Little ghosts playing and laughing and weeping on the edge of the southern memory can be a haunting thing. Surely one can reject a child one has brought into the world only by rejecting an equal part of one's psychic life, putting a sign over it and declaring it does not exist" (125). As an outward sign of white men's backyard relationships, these children are perceived as a threat to the "stable" social order and hence must be erased somehow. Smith continues, "It worked so well because the church and the home kept guilt and hate flowing into the reservoir, while the politician and business man had nothing to do but keep pumping it out" (122). People in power tapped into these traumas to keep fear alive for their own advantage, hence perpetuating the trauma.

Complicating the psychological weight of the ghosts produced from mixed-race sexual dynamics, many white children in the South were raised in part by black nurses. Smith writes, "This dual relationship which so many white southerners have had with two mothers, one white and one colored and each of a different culture that centered in different human values, makes the Oedipus complex seem by comparison almost a simple adjustment" (131). As the white child grows, the black mother so important to him is pushed away by society, supplanting her with the white mother and her pedestal. According to Smith, while this arrangement ostensibly reduced the weight of maternal responsibility for white mothers, it also alienated them from their children and themselves:

> Of all the humiliating experiences which southern white women have endured, the least easy to accept, I think, was that of a mother who had no choice but to take the husk of a love which her son in his earliest years had given to another woman.... It was as if these women never quite left the presence of the dead but mourned gently and continuously a loss they could not bear to know the extent of. (138)

That this legacy of rape, rejected children, and rejected mother figures is not recognized in "official" southern histories shows how deep these traumas run in southern society. The trauma is self-sustaining as the sins of the fathers are imposed on each subsequent generation. The historical trauma *is* the societal trauma, which maintains the dynamic's intergenerational nature.

In *Killers*, Smith discusses her own black nurse, who resides in her psyche like a ghost, exploring the psychological pressures on someone who meets a child's needs but is not seen as a valued relation, as opposed to a white mother who may not meet a child's needs but is seen as worthier of love. Smith tells the story of being handed over to Aunt Chloe, her nurse, when a younger child took her place as the baby of the family, and how Aunt Chloe was able to end a young Smith's food strike—by chewing the food for the child before feeding it to her. Smith writes, "Such a relationship with such a woman is not to be brushed off by the semantic trick of labelling her a 'nurse'" (130). She reflects on her relationship with Aunt Chloe, stating, "I knew but never believed it, that the deep respect I felt for her, the tenderness, the love, was a childish thing which every normal child outgrows ... and that somehow—though it seemed impossible to my agonized heart—I too, must outgrow these feelings" (29). The process of letting go of the caretaker to sustain the racial power structure wounds southerners deeply, both personally and societally.

Smith's strategy of examining these issues through her experience serves as a bridge for readers who fear confrontation with their own ghosts. Although most of *Killers* involves a precise dissection of the South, much of the book is also memoir, shedding light on the relationship between large-scale historical and societal trauma and the personal. Smith describes events from her childhood, showcasing not just personal traumas but intergenerational traumas. Jenkins states, "Some of her most vivid writing . . . relies on images of children, often conflated with memories of her own youth. If segregation represented for Smith the bifurcation of the adult personality, then the teaching or masking or explaining away of segregation began this splitting at a very early age" (121). In the anecdote of "the little white girl," Smith reveals that it fell on her to tell the girl, Janie, that she would be leaving the next day because white and black cannot live together. Although on some level Smith recognizes her parents' hypocrisy, she describes the guilt and anxiety that nonetheless plagued her as she considered that "for three weeks [she] had done things that white children were not supposed to do" (38). In addition to raising the question of what it means to be black or white when skin color is not a sufficient signifier, this story reveals that the trauma, for Smith and for southerners at large, is caused not by interracial interactions themselves but by the social disapproval of such integration. This experience was not traumatizing until the people involved perceived that Janie was not white. It was then that the pressures of the societal trauma set in. A white child had been playing, eating, and sleeping with a black one, and she had been told how bad this was, how sinful (38). The trauma surrounding these "ghost" relationships affected Smith personally and southern society as a whole, haunting the present and casting a cloud over the future. Smith writes, "So many of us are sleepwalkers wandering around in search of a past that never existed; more afraid of ghosts than of atomic war, gazing backward at a Civil War fought a century ago instead of looking into the cold eye of the storm bearing

Personal and Societal Trauma in *Killers of the Dream*   81

down on us" (18). Jenkins notes Smith's emphasis on the intergenerational effects of such repression: "Her writing brims with descriptions of children who are spiritually damaged before they can even define what race is and with white women who have become utterly detached from their own physical and spiritual presences. They float through her work like disembodied ghosts, pale, shriveled human voids" (113). Smith's strategic focus on children helps develop her argument that this trauma is passed from one generation to the next.

Killers of the Dream asserts that the difficult work of examining these traumas is necessary for healing and stopping the cycle. Elise Miller, in her article "Mourning and Melancholy: Literary Criticism by African American Women," states that "becoming a subject of— rather than being subjected to—history depends upon a capacity for empathy that does not slip into enervating entanglements with the past and its ghosts" (465). According to *Killers*, unless the cycle can be broken, society will continue to be plagued by these ghosts in the future. The *Killers of the Dream* are killers not only of the past and present but of the future as well.

Although she clearly *sees*, Smith expresses her fear, several times throughout *Killers*, that she may be a Cassandra, a prophetess in Greek mythology whose prophecies were always true but never believed. Discussing the link between colonialism and segregation in her foreword, Smith writes, "It is such an old story. The Cassandras have been giving out their warnings for years. But time has run out: we must, right now, adjust ourselves to the speed and quality of world events, world moods, world psychology, or face probable extinction as a free nation" (18). The traumas of the South and of the United States have made it easy to stagnate rather than act, caught in the cycle of "this is how things are done" and "we have no problems." The foreword, as well as the last two chapters added in a later edition of *Killers*, reveals that Smith's warning of the first edition was not heeded immediately after the book's initial publication.

In 1960, just before the revised edition of *Killers* was published, she voiced, in a letter to both Eugene Patterson and Jack Spalding, editors of the *Atlanta Constitution* and the *Atlanta Journal*, respectively, her fear that she was likely a Cassandra: "So once more, like dear old Cassandra, I must cry out a warning to my beloved people" (256). Emphasizing her skepticism that the warning would be heeded, she wrote in a letter to Dr. Paul Tillich in December of that year, "Sometimes as I write, talk, work[,] trying, like a Cassandra, to warn my people, I feel the words breaking to pieces against my face" (263). Yet, in an attempt to build on any momentum generated by the first edition of *Killers*, she implies, in a chapter added for the second edition, that sympathetic readers are not alone: "In the South—and once more, let's turn back to it—our big hope lies in the fact that ten years ago, only a few saw things clearly; now, thousands see. Not only the lonely individuals and the Cassandras, but groups—and these groups are growing larger and more energetic" (249).

A blending of realism and hope suffuses her writing concerning the present and the future. She recognizes the changes in her lifetime. However, the future haunts *Killers*, as Smith anticipates the South's resistance to giving up its ghosts: "So the South walked backwards into its future. It is no wonder people were hurt on the journey" (68). She reiterates her skepticism through the ominous words of a camper: "I don't like the future. It doesn't seem to belong to us" (55). Yet hope peeks through what might otherwise seem a fatalistic perspective, as Smith argues that time is of the essence. She warns, "If only we could afford this zigzagging walk into the future!" (252).

In the two chapters added in the revised edition of *Killers*, Smith characterizes the South's progress as "two steps forward, one step back." She acknowledges the beginnings of trauma processing in a culture generally resistant to self-analysis: "The old southern mold had cracked wide open and we had begun to see what it had done to us. . . . We were beginning to see how entwined are the white man's beliefs about sin and sex and segregation and money" (228). The atomic bomb, Smith observes, did spur a step backward into the safety of what was familiar: "We had been forced into a future that our feelings had no preparation for and our minds could only

Personal and Societal Trauma in *Killers of the Dream* 83

grasp crude approximations of. . . . We slammed doors in our mind; we scratched August 6 off of the world calendar; we began to build wispy shaky bridges to tie us to a past that no longer was there" (230). This is the zigzagging walk into the future Smith spoke of, where the traumas and ghosts are more comfortable than a living future. Under these conditions, the threads of sin, sex, and segregation retain their tight hold over the southern mind and culture. Nonetheless her commitment to naming and confronting this trauma belies Smith's hope that the South might do the work necessary to break the cycle.

She continues to urge that readers can secure the future by reclaiming their childhood to transform the ghosts of repression. In an October 2, 1964, letter to Phyllis Meras, a journalist who had interviewed Smith the year before, she writes, "Read the last chapter of the revised (1962) edition [and] you will see what I mean by man evolving into something far more complex, intense, *thinking.* . . . He is in a very real sense . . . participating in his own evolution by the tensions set up by his own discoveries and thoughts" (310; italics in original). In *Killers of the Dream*, Smith expresses her belief that human connection and understanding can stop the cycle of trauma and restore the future; she writes:

I believe every creative act, every poem, every painting, every honest question or honest dissent, every gesture of courage and faith and mercy and concern will count; every new awareness will count; every time we defend the human spirit it will count; every time we turn away from arrogance and lies, this, [too], will count in the project called *Human Being Evolving.* (239; italics in original)

Through the realizing and processing of trauma at all levels and the reclaiming of childhood, the cycle can end. The South must pick through the threads of sin, sex, and segregation as Smith has done, examining the effects on the individual, society, and future generations. Smith cautions that this evolution will not be instantaneous, and it will not be comfortable. The struggle to emerge from trauma is the struggle to let go of the familiar, as these traumas are ingrained in the landscape, the culture, and the history of the South. The wound originates in the South, so the healing too must come from it.

Discussions of place and a sense of place exist throughout Balaev's discussion of trauma, showing the importance of the location of the traumatic event or events. She writes, "Descriptions of the geographic place of traumatic experience and remembrance situate the individual in relation to a larger cultural context that contains social values that influence the recollection of the event and reconfiguration of the self" ("Trends" 149). As someone who remained committed to the South despite its traumas, Smith offers hope to the reader through her willingness to grapple with the dense fabric and ghosts of the wounded culture.

The entirety of *Killers* strikes a balance between hope and criticism of the region Smith called home. As Margaret Rose Gladney and Lisa Hodgens describe in their introduction to selections from *Killers*, "Combining personal memoir, allegory, and direct social commentary, no other work so effectively psychoanalyzed the South's rigid commitment to racial segregation" (157). Although psychoanalysis requires painful confrontation with the subconscious, it also implies the possibility of healing and growth. In the final lines of *Killers*, Smith writes:

> And now, I must break off this story that has not ended; a story that is, after all, only one small fragment, hardly more than a page in a big book where is being recorded what happened to men and women and children of the earth during the Great Ordeal when finally they separated themselves a little way from nature and assumed the burden of their own evolution. (253)

Though the final chapters of *Killers* showcase the work being done against segregation, particularly the civil rights movement, Smith realizes that we still have much work to do. The large-scale societal and historical traumas will take time to heal, as will the personal and intergenerational wounds, but the outcome now lies in the hands of the people. Although the psychological and social fabric of the South still contains threads of sin, sex, and segregation, Smith urges us to face our ghosts and embrace the possibility of a healthier future.

Note

1. Interest in the insights that trauma theory brings to the study of southern literature is increasing, seen in publications such as Lisa Hinrichsen's *Possessing the South: Trauma, Imagination, and Memory in Post-plantation Southern Literature* (2015) and "Trauma Studies and the Literature of the U.S. South," as well as Michał Choiński's *Southern Hyperboles: Metafigurative Strategies of Narration.*

Works Cited

Balaev, Michelle. "Literary Trauma Theory Reconsidered." *Contemporary Approaches in Literary Trauma Theory*, edited by Michelle Balaev, Palgrave Macmillan, 2014, pp. 1–14.

Balaev, Michelle. "Trends in Literary Trauma Theory." *Mosaic: An Interdisciplinary Critical Journal*, vol. 41, no. 2, 2008, pp. 149–66.

Choiński, Michał. *Southern Hyperboles: Metafigurative Strategies of Narration.* Louisiana State UP, 2020.

Gladney, Margaret Rose, ed. *How Am I to Be Heard? Letters of Lillian Smith.* U of North Carolina P, 1993.

Gladney, Margaret Rose. Introduction. *Killers of the Dream*, by Lillian Smith, Norton, 1994, n.p.

Gladney, Margaret Rose, and Lisa Hodgens, eds. *A Lillian Smith Reader.* U of Georgia Press, 2016.

Hinrichsen, Lisa. *Possessing the South: Trauma, Imagination, and Memory in Post-plantation Southern Literature.* Louisiana State UP, 2015.

Hinrichsen, Lisa. "Trauma Studies and the Literature of the U.S. South." *Literature Compass*, vol. 10, no. 8, 2013, pp. 605–17.

Jenkins, McKay. "Metaphors of Race and Psychological Damage in the 1940s American South: The Writings of Lillian Smith." *Racing and (E)racing Language: Living with the Color of Our Words*, edited by Ellen J. Goldner and Safiya Henderson-Holmes, Syracuse UP, 2001, pp. 99–123.

Miller, Elise. "Mourning and Melancholy: Literary Criticism by African American Women." *Tulsa Studies in Women's Literature*, vol. 35, no. 2, 2016, pp. 463–89.

Myrdal, Gunnar. *An American Dilemma: The Negro Problem and Modern Democracy.* Harper & Brothers, 1944.

Smith, Lillian. *Killers of the Dream*. Norton, 1994.

Smith, Lillian. Letter to Eugene Patterson and Jack Spalding, October 22, 1960. Gladney, pp. 254–56.

Smith, Lillian. Letter to George Reynolds, February 14, 1940. Gladney, pp. 35–41.

Smith, Lillian. Letter to Marianne Fink, May 2, 1961. Gladney, pp. 271–75.

Smith, Lillian. Letter to Paul Tillich, December 1960. Gladney, pp. 261–64.

Smith, Lillian. Letter to Phyllis L. Meras, October 2, 1964. Gladney, pp. 309–11.

Smith, Lillian. "Report from Lillian Smith on *Killers of the Dream*." Gladney, pp. 127–32.

Smith, Lillian. "A Southerner Talking, November 27, 1948." Gladney and Hodgens, pp. 147–48.

Watson, Jay. "Uncovering the Body, Discovering Ideology: Segregation and Sexual Anxiety in Lillian Smith's *Killers of the Dream*." *American Quarterly*, vol. 49, no. 3, 1997, pp. 470–503.

persistent criticism of the Agrarians and their descendants the New Critics, then firmly ensconced in academic departments and editorial positions in major literary magazines, where they remained for at least a decade after Smith's death. Her most famous books, *Strange Fruit* and *Killers of the Dream*, were often overlooked in studies of southern literature,[1] and her many other works—Smith published five additional full-length books and numerous essays—and other interests were rarely discussed at all. As analyses of Smith's work have slowly accumulated over the last forty years, critics have also made a persistent but often unanswered call to consider Smith's literary artistry and feminism. Anne C. Loveland's preface to her 1986 biography of Smith observes, "Nevertheless, the tendency so far has been to focus on her work in the Civil Rights movement and to neglect her literary effort. Both aspects of her career are important. More than anything, Lillian wanted to be recognized as a creative writer and thinker" (2). Margaret Rose Gladney, in the introduction to her 1993 selection of Smith's letters, *How Am I to Be Heard?*, makes a similar comment regarding Smith's negotiations with gender prescriptions: "Neither biographers, historians, nor literary critics, however, have seriously examined the full burden of [Smith's] struggle as a woman living and writing in the Deep South in the five decades between the two feminist movements of the twentieth century" (xiv). I hope to contribute at least one step down this little-traveled path by considering Smith's characterization of Susie, the "poor mad" motel operator's wife in Smith's 1954 work *The Journey*.

Described by Will Brantley as a "a philosophical meditation that grew out of a trip she took back to the small Florida town of her youth" (48), the book parallels Smith's journey through coastal Georgia and Florida with her search for "an image of the human being that I could feel proud of" to counter the one that had been "trampled down, flattened by totalitarian beliefs that we are not aware we hold, torn by the Censors who fatten on our fears; made conforming, 'normal,' animal-like, machinelike, absolute" (6). While race is certainly a part of her discussion, as it is inextricably related to all matters of

CHAPTER 4

Martha, Mary, and Susie: Totalitarian Political Ideology and Women in Lillian Smith's *The Journey*

—Wendy Kurant Rollins

The work of Lillian Smith is ripe for reconsideration, especially because it was never fully considered in the first place. As she was painfully aware, Smith's expertise and writing were frequently minimized to an exclusive focus on the racial problems of the South or even ignored outright. In a 1957 letter to her friend Lawrence Kubie, Smith fumes about a network talk show's cowardly curtailing of her commentary on segregation and then observes that this reception of her and her work is pervasive:

> This smothering has crept into quite a few odd places: for instance, if somebody writes about best-sellers in this country during the past fifteen years, *Strange Fruit* is never mentioned; although it broke, as you know, ALL RECORDS for a serious book. If race books are mentioned, I am never included. Yet my books on the problems of race and segregation have sold more than those of any other writer in the world. (218)

If the popular press's silence on even her most well-known works can be explained by its timidity in the face of consumer backlash, the same behavior on the part of literary circles might be traced to Smith's

Totalitarian Political Ideology and Women in *The Journey*   89

southern culture, *The Journey* focuses more on the South's addiction to totalitarian political views and leaders and, very similarly to *Killers of the Dream*, traces its origins in psychological wounds sustained in childhood, as well as its consequences for southerners laboring under it. At the book's physical center is Smith's encounter with two extremely different motel operators with whom she interacts during her trip; the first, Cephas, is the very model of the southern demagogue's prime supporter. Cephas has received a small amount of critical attention, though sometimes it is nothing further than the singular observation that Smith in this book "revealed a special talent for describing motel operators, in their different species, who she had met on her tour" (Blackwell and Clay 107). His wife Susie, with whom Smith also interacts, has received none. However, Susie is worth consideration. Smith weaves into Susie's characterization two sides or impulses that Smith frequently identified in herself and called her Martha and Mary sides. In doing so, Smith lays bare the maddening and isolating effects of totalitarian political culture on women and adds to a discussion of women's experience in the South started in *Killers of the Dream*.

To understand Smith's diagnosis of negative psychological effects, it is useful to know what she considers psychologically optimal. Smith's context is the Jungian construction of the psyche and its primary orientation parameters of extraversion and introversion. For Jung, the human psyche was composed of the interactive components of the ego (the center of conscious awareness), the personal unconscious (mostly consistent with Freud's view of the same, though Jung argued that it contained more than repressed feelings), and the collective unconscious (a repository of knowledge accumulated by the experiences of humanity through time and structured by key themes called archetypes). While the interactions of these different parts of the psyche could shift, an individual's personality would tend toward either extraversion or introversion, which indicated whether objective or subjective reality dictated his or her perspective. With extraversion, "orientation by the object predominates" (Casement 63), and so the extraverted individual leans more heavily on the rational mind, in which the ego makes judgments about external reality. In comparison, "The introvert derives its conscious attitude from the realm of the collective unconscious. . . . These subjective tendencies are taken to be identical with the object by the individual experiencing them" (Casement 66). This latter is the mythic mind; it tends to see external reality only in the ways through which it conforms to the subjective structure of a particular archetype. For this kind of mind, external reality is a symbol of the mind's internal reality. Smith follows Jung in asserting that the individual needs a balance of these dichotomies for both a healthy psyche and a healthy society. In her 1961 expansion of the chapter "The Chasm and the Bridge" in *Killers*, Smith calls for leaders "who understand the difference in facts and symbols and can keep from merging their mythic with their rational mind" (243).[2] In *The Journey*, Smith calls these leaders "quality folks," playing on and subverting the usual implications of the term: quality folks are "not 'aristocracy,' not 'rich people,' not the learned, not the white race, not people who happen to have ancestors who understood honor and accepted responsibility but people *who themselves* have learned the meaning of these words and the quality they give a man's relationships not only with other people but with himself" (224). Though she does not use the terminology of the mythic and rational minds in the "quality folks" discussion, her two descriptions overlap. "Quality folks" are quality because they both understand the abstract and mythic concepts of honor and responsibility and can make them objective truths through their interactions with others.

The South's problems arise from a lack of balance through overemphasis on the mythic mind. Smith observes that southerners "mingle symbols and facts as if they were molasses and feathers" (*Killers* 243), referencing a distraction used by adults to keep children occupied. Furthermore, Smith notes that, in southerners spooked by social change after World War II, "mythic thinking superseded reason" (*Killers* 230). Individuals dominated by the mythic mind tend to forget one of Jung's key observations about the myths it produces;

they are "symbolic of a process taking place in the mind, not in the world" (Segal 67). Southerners' mingling of symbols projected by the mythic mind and facts that should be assessed by the rational mind leads them to treat symbols "as though they are facts"; molasses fuses with feather, never to be separated again. Furthermore, the mythic mind out of control has an effect that has much in common with the mechanisms of a totalitarian system:

> The mythic mind is not capable of relating: its *modus operandi* is one of spreading: it is not restrained by the barriers of time and space, or cause and effect, or facts that contradict, or logical categories. . . . It likes to create something big out of the small: it can take one quality, such as whiteness, and cover a neighborhood or a quarter of the earth with it, declaring that all beneath this great white sheet are the "same." (*Killers* 245)

In *The Journey*, the character who most illustrates Smith's description of a southerner held in thrall by the all-encompassing mythic mind is Cephas, the manager of a motor court at which Smith spends the night during her titular travels.

Cephas's role in *The Journey* is clear: he "prepares the way for [Smith's] notion of 'quality folks' by dramatizing its opposite. . . . Bad taste, naïve faith in the 'modrun,' ignorance of what makes folks 'quality,' lack of honor, and fear and hatred of un-American others form a seamless whole" (Haddox 57). He is the same type of southerner Smith atomized in the first edition of *Killers*, just with a veneer of commodity capitalism and Cold War–era anticommunist virulence added. Showing Smith her room at the motor court, Cephas boasts, "Everything in the place is modrun," and displays the magnificence of the "mauve-colored lavatory and the mauve-colored toilet and mauve-colored toilet paper" (*Journey* 88). His delight in these consumer items is accompanied by disdainful remarks about higher education, and Smith wonders whether he is aware of "the intelligence, the persistence and patience and rigorous honesty of the scientific method"

92   Wendy Kurant Rollins

that contributed to the creation of these products. She decides that he does not: "However they got here, he knows that they are *things that money can buy.* That money cannot create them any more than it can make the earth and the forests and the sea and the rivers, or a human being, would seem to him incredible" (89). Despite his "modrun" amenities, Cephas demonstrates the same old mythic-mind tendencies of white supremacist thinking. As they chat outside in the motor court's parking lot, a car pulls in, and its black passengers quickly take the measure of Cephas's baleful glare, retreating immediately. As Smith asserts in her additions to *Killers,* southerners "are still fixed on old fears; our demagogues at home and in Congress are still wailing about mixing and mongrelizing and 'our way of life' and the 'outsiders' and the 'agitators'" (241). The only new twist is that now communists can be blamed. Cephas accordingly grumbles at the retreating car that "somebody better run them Communists out of this country quick. If they don't—see what will happen?" (*Journey* 94). The mythic mind, whether it is ignoring the facts about how consumer items are developed or imposing the symbolism of racial and political purity on all human interactions, is clearly in charge in Cephas.

Smith also uses Cephas to demonstrate that, regardless of his expressions of passionate hatred of communists, he would not hesitate to use their methods because they are the methods of the dominating mythic mind. As noted earlier, Smith asserted that the mythic mind does not relate; it spreads and remakes things in the image of its reigning archetype. Similarly, Cephas, through his idol Joseph McCarthy, wants to remake American institutions in his image of ideological purity. Directly after showing Smith the amenities of his motel, Cephas gleefully anticipates that his idol will "clean out the schools and the colleges and all the Communist professors and them scientists," and additionally asserts that "every Communist and Catholic," as well as Jews, "ought to be run out of the country" (*Journey* 89). He returns to his favorite theme after the brief threat of being integrated: "They tell me the Kremlin's got em everywhere—in our schools and churches, everywhere. Only thing to do is take every book and go through it word for word and clean it out. Clean em all out!" When Smith observes that this would be time-consuming, Cephas offers up a solution: "O.K. Then burn em. Burn them all up" (*Journey* 94). Cephas's advocacy of the tactics of Nazi Germany and communist Russia (and Joseph McCarthy) cements the common origin of these otherwise different political ideologies: the totalitarian imposition of the mythic mind over the materials of rationality; if something does not fit with the mythic mind's prized archetype, then it must be obliterated. Smith was perhaps aware of John Milton's famous comment on the motives of a book burner: "He who destroys a good book kills reason." Ultimately, southerners like Cephas are not anticommunist because they object to communism's tactics; they hate it because "Communism challenges their own brand of authoritarianism" (Brinkmeyer 144). Again, Cephas is entirely oblivious of the irony in his comments, but Smith is not: "Though he hates 'the Communists' because they take away man's freedom, he, too, would like to liquidate all people who differ from him" (*Journey* 90).

The little critical attention the Cephas chapter has received rarely includes a consideration of his wife Susie, though Smith spends at least equal time on thoughts of and interaction with her. Additionally, Smith considered the Susie conversation significant enough that she wanted to include it in her audio recording of excerpts from her work. In her December 9, 1965, letter to Margaret Sullivan, Smith mentions Joan Titus borrowing an "elegant machine" from Time Life Broadcast and making recordings in Smith's bedroom (337–38). Smith has plans for more recordings when her sister Esther arrives for a visit: "Then Esther and I want to do the Miss Susie scene from *The Journey.* . . . While she is here, maybe we'll make on my machine (not really a bad one) the Miss Susie scene, Esther doing the wacky, mad Miss Susie while I do myself, the commentator" (338). Another reason to delve further into Susie's characterization is that Smith herself claimed a special expertise in understanding women's experiences. In a 1962 letter to Rochelle Girson, the book review editor for the *Saturday Review*, for which Smith sometimes wrote, Smith urges:

> Do give me a chance at some female stuff now and then; I hate to be stereotyped as a race specialist or Civil [Rights] specialist or South specialist. I do know a goodish bit about such matters but what I really know best is women and their curvatures of soul and twisting relationships. . . . I am part Mary and part Martha: as Martha, I have written about segregation, the South, etc., etc.; as Mary, I know best girls, women, artists. (*How* 295)

Furthermore, the juxtaposition of Smith's claim of expertise about women's lives and her description of herself having Martha and Mary sides implies a relation between the two and gives us a lens through which to examine Susie's characterization.

Smith is alluding to the Martha and Mary story of the Gospel, a story that was extremely significant to Smith's view of herself, her work, and ultimately her depiction of Susie. The story, which appears in the tenth chapter of the book of Luke, traces some of Jesus's teachings as he travels from Galilee to Jerusalem, and follows the parable of the Good Samaritan, which is also relevant to Susie's characterization. The parable is told in response to a question of who should be considered a neighbor when loving one's neighbor as one's self, so the choice of a Samaritan as the exemplar asserts that one's neighbors include even people traditionally seen as opponents. Many commentators argue that the beleaguered traveler was likely a Jew, and Jews and Samaritans are represented as holding one another in low esteem in other parts of the Bible. The Samaritan puts aside a long history of rivalry to show kindness to the injured traveler, suggesting that the hearers of the lesson should do no less. The parable is immediately followed by the story of Martha and Mary:

> A certain woman named Martha received [Jesus] into her house.
> And she had a sister called Mary, which also sat at Jesus' feet and heard his word.

Totalitarian Political Ideology and Women in *The Journey*   95

> But Martha was cumbered about much serving, and came to him, and said, Lord, dost thou not care that my sister hath left me to serve alone? Bid her therefore that she help me.
>
> And Jesus answered and said unto her, Martha, Martha, thou art careful and troubled about many things:
>
> But one thing is needful: and Mary hath chosen that good part, which shall not be taken away from her. (Luke 10:38–42 KJV)

Common interpretations of the story hold that it symbolizes "the tension between the contemplative and the active dimensions in the life of all Christians and of the Church," with Mary representing "the contemplative" and Martha representing "the active and apostolic aspect" (Dale and Smith 628). Others have seen the tale as speaking "to those who spend their lives working hard but who lose track of those things which are most important" or "to those who give themselves generously but feel unappreciated" (629). It is a story that often elicits strong personal reactions, according to John Dale and Christian Smith, and it is one that Smith cited in her reflections on her own nature numerous times throughout her life.

"Martha and Mary have been fighting inside me since I was fifteen," Smith told the Harcourt Brace Jovanovich editor Dan Wickenden in 1961, and though the meanings she attached to the two sides were multiple, the two figures consistently represented the conflict between responding to the needs of others and exploring her own interests (*How* 285). Early in her adult life, "The Martha side was her conscience that commanded her to give up her own freedom and interests to help her family," specifically to assist her parents in running their north Georgia girls' camp and in nursing her mother through her illnesses after her father's death.[3] Conversely, "The Mary side of her nature represented self-indulgence and freedom.... Thus her music and, even more, her writing became a means of obtaining the freedom and pleasure the Martha side denied her" (Loveland 20). Eventually Smith used the story to represent conflicting pulls within her writing subject matter, though, good Jungian that she was, she hoped to finally integrate them and satisfy both sides' demands.

In an unpublished autobiographical sketch written in 1964, Smith described her negotiation with her overzealous Martha side when deciding to start a literary magazine:[4]

> Martha stepped in and said, pushing my conscience hard, "While you are doing this, you must face up to all the implications of what this southern way of life is. You must do something to change things." . . . I sighed. "Do I always have to stop my dreaming and creating to mop up messes? I've done the home messes, do I now have to do the South's dirty work?" Martha was adamant. . . . Yes, I had to help. I could still create but I also had to help. . . . Not by organization work . . . but maybe by giving insight, maybe by trying to "see the whole tree"— maybe I could show the roots now hidden by the old southern myths and half-lies and rationalizations and defenses. (Qtd. in Loveland 26)

Smith's ideal accommodation between her two sides was to write nonfiction that "intermingled imagination and mythic mind with reason and fact," achieving the same balanced psyche she attributes to "quality folks" in *The Journey*, so that her work was just "as creative and full of art and poetry as fiction" (Loveland 235). As she described it to Bruce Galphin of the *Atlanta Constitution*, "Mary slips inside Martha and shows her how to take the human 'problems' and transmute them into poetry and art of a sort, at least; and maybe, now and then, into something really valid and enduring" (qtd. in Loveland 235). It was a balance she struggled to sustain.

Smith sometimes despaired that her Mary side would ever get its fair share of recognition, both from herself and from those who judged her work. Prefacing her hope for a true Martha-Mary balance in her Galphin letter, Smith admits, "The 'Martha' in me . . . is always pushing the 'Mary' aside to clean up the messes, to feed the starving" (Loveland 235). Smith sensed that this internal tendency was reinforced by external expectations. While the Gospel prioritizes Mary's choice, the world consistently demands that women devote themselves to Martha's work. In the aforementioned letter to Wickenden,

Smith laments, "It is a losing battle for Mary (with whom I am more deeply identified) I am afraid, but I always keep hoping that I can be myself, write the way I want to, do what I want to—and not what everybody else seems to need of me" (285). Four years later, again fighting the cancer that would end her life in 1966, her hope that her Mary side would be acknowledged had significantly diminished. Smith was named the first recipient of the Queen Esther Scroll from the National Women's Division of the American Jewish Congress, but her pleasure in the award was assailed by how the press represented the award, as she told Kubie in a letter on April 5, 1965. She wrote, "I was given it for my 'creative genius,' which pleased me; but the press[,] determined to diminish me, changed it to an award for her 'courage and commitment.' They have stereotyped me as a propagandist and friend of the Negro Cause and they are determined that I not be looked at as an important writer." She calls the deliberate refusal to acknowledge her creativity, the skill allied with her Mary side, "the unhealing wound of my life" (*How* 320).[5]

Smith had previously explored the impact of the racial status quo on southern white women in "The Women" chapter of *Killers of the Dream*. Susie's characterization suggests that Smith continued to explore the effects of ideology—this time capitalism and demagoguery—on women's Martha and Mary impulses. Susie's Martha side is first emphasized in her name, an allusion to another woman who hosted Jesus in the book of Luke, "Susanna . . . which ministered unto him of [her] substance" (Luke 8:3 KJV). As we have seen in Smith's own application of the Martha model to herself, Martha's focus particularly is on "mop[ping] up messes" and "feed[ing] the starving" (Loveland 26, 235), and these qualities are also emphasized in Susie's characterization. Before we see Susie in person, Cephas tells Smith that one of Susie's main activities is "cleaning up the rooms" of the motel; she is "a great one for keeping things spic and span" and turns to reading the Bible only "when she can't find no more dust." Another major activity is "cooking over at the house," the yields of which she makes a point of sharing with the motel's last Sunday guest.

Smith is the lucky recipient during her stay. Cephas tells her, "Every Sunday night she sends over a little something for the last traveler who comes our way. She calls it her Good Samaritan deed," and so, as in Luke, Martha is juxtaposed closely with the Good Samaritan. However, Susie's Samaritan-Martha impulses are hampered by her husband's devotion to consumer capitalism. Cephas admits that his wife is "mighty proud of their motor court but making money troubled her," observing, "All her life, her daddy welcomed the stranger and never charged a cent to nobody for spending the night. They was someone to welcome, she was always saying, not to take money from. And how do you know you might not be sheltering an angel unawares?" Cephas laughs at his wife's "notions," implying they are something congenitally female and therefore out of touch with real life, and commenting, "If Susie saw the whisky bottles I take out of those rooms before she goes to clean, she'd not worry much about angels" (*Journey* 91). The question of why, if he finds her naive, he doesn't let her encounter those whisky bottles herself is left unasked.

The effects of Cephas's demagoguery are introduced in a dream Smith has on the night she spends in the motel. Likely inspired by Cephas's paranoia that "the Kremlin's got em everywhere," Smith dreams of Susie and herself "in Moscow—and Susie was carrying a pitcher of ice lemonade and a slice of marble cake to the Kremlin looking for the last weary traveler" (*Journey* 94, 96). Just as the Good Samaritan put aside a contentious history to help a member of a rival group, so Susie seeks to extend hospitality to the icon of America's Cold War enemy, regardless of whether the weary traveler within might be a "fellow traveler" or more. The dream shows Susie's Martha impulse again stifled as her search for a recipient of her hospitality becomes a McCarthy-style hearing:

> But there were so many, and all had to be questioned, and we could not decide who was the last one, really. For the Inquisitors had turned into little gator-frogs sitting around A Very Big Table, and they were roaring like jet planes—and you could not think, you could not decide

anything. So we turned away and Susie wept because she could not carry out her Good Samaritan deed. (*Journey* 96)

First, one must pause to appreciate Smith's sly dig at McCarthy and his acolytes. Here they are just little frogs—more specifically, those commonly known as pig frogs—who make noises like much more fearsome beasts, perhaps to conceal how vulnerable they are themselves. Pathetic as they are, they nonetheless are effective at confounding Susie's Martha mission, and the consequences for her are not so amusing. After Susie's tearful failure, the dream ends with the two "on a beach and all around us was Susie's loneliness and the only sound on earth was a music thin as a gull's cry that floated out of a starfish softly turning, turning in wet sand" (96). Susie starts with the intention of loving her neighbor and ends up isolated, her powerlessness reinforced by the ineffectually turning starfish, a symbol frequently associated with another biblical example of a loving woman, the Virgin Mary. The strains of Béla Bartók's sonata for solo violin, described by Smith as making "a cold sound to the heart" (*Journey* 96), provide the soundtrack of her isolation and sadness.

Susie's Mary side fares even more disastrously, its impulses distorted into arrested development, psychosis, and a desire for destruction. The depiction of Mary sitting at Jesus's feet and listening to his teaching is evoked in Smith's description of children at the conclusion of Cephas and Susie's chapter. Children abound with "hungry questions . . . like little puppies, sniffing, tasting, trying out the world." Their questions eventually modulate into a desire for stories: "If you cannot tell me the first and last chapters of my life, then tell me another story, almost anything will do" (*Journey* 102). When Smith finally meets Susie in person, she sees Susie as a child, with "eyes, big and unmoving, like a child when listening to a story that must not end. Ageless eyes. Ageless face. Time had stopped for Susie. Even her body had guessed it for it was caught in amber-like stillness" (98). In her concluding remarks on the loss of childhood questioning, Smith attributes the loss to children's partial starvation—they are fed with only "a few scraps of half-lies and half-facts; and now and then wonderful ghost stories, or laughter, or silence"—and "slow-creeping shame" (103). Susie's retention of her childlike qualities is somehow worse than the usual process of loss Smith describes. With Susie, her childlike qualities are presented not as evergreen youthfulness but as an uncanny embalmment. She had a "face like wax" with "yellowed smooth translucent skin," and Smith cannot imagine that "a heart beat or blood moved even a slow inch" within Susie (98). The child hungry to learn has been frozen in a sort of living death. Worse still, rather than either losing that hunger or feeding it with imagination and creativity as Smith has, Susie has turned to maladaptive sources of nourishment that Smith compares to geophagy, noting in the chapter's conclusion that "the mind loses its hunger for truth if it is never fed it when young, and turns to strange substitutes as does the little clay-eater whose body, craving a balanced diet which it does not receive, develops an insatiable appetite for dirt" (103). Susie's clay eating is her hallucinations of children and, when that too is rejected by those around her, her longing for the Apocalypse.

Much as her own Mary side finds fulfillment in imagination and creativity, Smith characterizes Susie as exercising her imagination to feed her Mary side in the form of imagining children playing in a magnolia tree behind the motel. In the earlier conversation between Smith and Cephas, magnolia trees came up in the context of reminiscing about their childhoods, "curiously alike, however different the houses our families had lived in" (93). When Smith remarks that the big magnolia she climbed as a child was likely not as big as her memory suggested, Cephas says, "Biggest I know is one in back of our house, over there. My wife'd be mighty proud to show it to you in the morning. Folks come miles to see it. It's more than a hundred years old" (*Journey* 93). Dutifully, Smith goes to look at the tree the next morning and meets Susie in person for the first time there. Without preamble, Susie describes to Smith the imaginary children she sees playing in the tree:

Totalitarian Political Ideology and Women in *The Journey*   101

"They're there, this morning," she said, "every last one of them. No use to listen, you won't hear them, they don't talk, they just play. Some have been in there since it was a little biddy tree and there's one over here who has been playing all by hisself nearbout eighty years on that same branch and two who have been—no, not there over here—sixty-four years, no sixty-three—Do you understand what I am saying?" she demanded with a fierce need to know. (*Journey* 98)

However, Susie's exercise of imagination is again distorted. The children she imagines are voiceless, stuck in the same place doing the same thing for decades, and often alone. This aspect of Susie resembles one of the reactions to the South's racial divisions that Smith discusses in "The Women" chapter of *Killers of the Dream*. "Unable to look at the ugly facts of their life," a small percentage of southern white women "learned to see mysterious things the rest of us could not see." The loss of their children's affection to a "mammy" and the loss of their sensuality to an ideal of "sacred womanhood" designed to bolster a racist status quo led them to see visions of more loss: "I remember how they 'felt' premonitions, counting shadows and making of them cryptic answers. They 'dreamed' that a beloved one would die and the beloved sometimes died. They 'felt' there would be no returning when one left on a long journey and sometimes there was no return" (*Killers* 139). Like Susie, these women experience life as death.

These stuck and silent children are one of Susie's few imaginative productions, but ironically, they only add to her loneliness. Susie's "fierce need to know" whether Smith understands that there are children in the tree is a result of her family's refusal to accept her vision. When Smith answers affirmatively, Susie continues, "I might uv knowed you'd know. But Cephas can't see them. I keep trying to explain and when he won't even try to see them you can understand why I had to slap him, can't you?" (*Journey* 98). Susie's imaginative outlet and her frustration that she cannot share it are interpreted as madness by her family, and they "sent [her] away. . . . To that place." Additionally, her family isolates her further by limiting her interactions with the real children in her life, her grandchildren. Susie speaks bitterly of her daughter-in-law: "She thinks I'll hurt *hers*. . . . Many a time I'd be real glad to baby-set but Grace says *No, she might hurt the kids*. She means *me*" (99). The tragedy of her family's decision is that they have cut Susie off from the only people around her likely to understand and accept her in her childlike state.

Like Smith, Susie wishes to integrate her Martha and Mary sides but struggles to articulate what she wants. While "staring at the ground" around her magnolia tree, Susie expresses fragments of her desires that Smith's sympathetic responses tease out (*Journey* 100). Smith understands finally that Susie wishes that "the ground was a piece of glass" so that she could see both the aboveground and underground parts of it at once:

"If only it was a piece of glass," she whispered.

"What, Susie?"

"Cause if it was—" She shook her head.

"What, Susie?"

"If it was, then all of it would be together. You know!" Her voice was sharp.

"You mean we could see the whole tree, then?" (*Journey* 102)

In this conversation with Susie, Smith gives us a proto-version of "the whole tree" that she would use as an image for her integration of Martha and Mary in the autobiographical sketch written ten years later. While Smith's later version acknowledges that she must actively work to "show the roots now hidden by the old southern myths and half-lies and rationalizations and defenses" (Loveland 26), Susie's more passive wish—it is the ground, not she, that needs to act—indicates her doubt about her abilities to achieve what she wants. The mental block has a familiar source, indicated by Susie's response to Smith's statement articulating Susie's wish:

She smiled. "I might uv knowed he couldn't see it. You know what?"

"What, Susie?" I felt I would never escape her world now.

"I've never had no use for no man cep'n two in all the world. My daddy and God." (*Journey* 102)

Cephas is notably not included, implying that his inability to see what Susie sees or to understand what she wants impedes her from finding a way to unify her impulses. Of course, he cannot see Susie's children; his mythic mind cannot relate to a symbol of learning and change because his dominating symbol insists on everything remaining the same as it has always been (toilet paper excepted). As Smith leaves to continue on her journey, Susie presses on her a gift that is perhaps Susie's one successful integration of her Martha impulse toward hospitality and her Mary impulse toward imaginative creation. Susie gives Smith "a little glass of mayhaw jelly," and as "the sun touched it . . . a thousand red and yellow lights spilled out of it" (*Journey* 100). Mayhaw jelly is a perfect symbol of the integration of these sometimes opposing impulses. Like cranberries and rhubarb, mayhaw alone is too tart for most people to enjoy; making it into jelly unites the tart and the sweet, just as a gift of beautiful food extends both hospitality and aesthetic pleasure.

Making jelly can only do so much to relieve Susie's frustrations. She longs for the Apocalypse and in that wish resembles another type of female reaction to toxic ideology described in *Killers of the Dream*. In that work, Smith describes a type of woman who resents and resists the gender conventions that buttress the South's racial conventions but who eventually "acquire[s], as do subjugated people who protest their chains, the more unpleasant qualities of their enemy" (*Killers* 140). In the case of the women in *Killers*, they adopt a contempt for the feminine. With Susie, she adopts and extends her husband's totalitarian desire to "burn them all up" and cleanse the world of his enemies. As Cephas tells Smith when she first arrives, Susie "knows Revelations by heart" and "sets up the whole night, sometimes, watching the stars" for signs that the "end of time" is near (*Journey* 91, 94, 95). Susie herself expresses her longing in the course of the conversation by the tree. After telling Smith of her attack on

Cephas and subsequent time in the hospital, Susie fears that Cephas is preparing to send her back to "that place" again. In response to Smith's demurral that the hospital might help her, Susie replies, "Only thing that can help me feel better is the end of time," and describes her anticipation, merging it with part of Revelations: "And when it comes I'll clap my hands and shout hallelujah and the voice of the seventh angel will begin to sound and the woman was given two wings of a great eagle that she might fly into the wilderness, into her place . . . where she is nourished for a time and times and half a time, from the face of the serpent" (*Journey* 99; Revelations 12:14 KJV). Susie's choice of this particular part of the passage suggests that she feels persecuted in her current environment—specifically by her husband—and looks forward to the end of times to whisk her away to a more nurturing place. However, much like her husband, in wishing for those who oppose her to be wiped from existence, she adopts the strategies of the enemy.

As her earlier dream of Susie foreshadowed, Smith's interaction with Susie ends on a pessimistic note. As Smith departs, she tells Susie that she is "looking for something . . . that is very important to [her] to find," and Susie implores, "bring it by and show me" (*Journey* 100, 101). Smith describes Susie's voice as she makes this request as "weak and small like the last cry for help of the medium's daughter in Menotti's opera." In *The Medium*, the daughter's love is fatally shot by her paranoid mother, another doppelgänger for Cephas and his "Kremlin's got em everywhere" thinking. There is no hope for the daughter or for Susie either. Smith predicts, "Soon now, they will take her back to That Place. Yes. A day will come when she will not have the strength or courage or hope or desire to do her Good Samaritan deed another time—and then? Then she may throw the lemonade in Cephas's face. And they will come for her so she cannot harm him or Grace's children" (101). Even the small accommodation of her Martha side will fail to make up for the more pervasive suppression of her Mary side, and her family will send her away, free from any harm she can do and ignorant of the harm they have done to her.

Totalitarian Political Ideology and Women in *The Journey*   105

While Susie's story seems destined for a tragic ending, *The Journey* is not a pessimistic book. Her story is quickly followed by indications of paths of escape. As Smith drives away from Cephas's motel, she reflects on her own childhood and how she escaped the repression of her Mary side. She, like other children, experienced the silence and misinformation that suppress "hungry questions." However,

> A time came, in these young years, when I grew skeptical of my schoolmates' explanations and of Frashy's big lies and of the silence of the grownups. The old questions were hurting again. I was longing for "the truths" as I had hungered for it when two, three, four years old—only now, I asked the questions in different words, and did not go to people for the answers. I began to make purposeful trips to that upstairs room [the family library]. Then it was, that I found Shakespeare. (*Journey* 120)

Subsequently she "discovered Bach and Beethoven and Chopin and Schumann (and a few others, of course, as odd as the old dusty authors in our library) for there was a music teacher. And she was . . . the Good Teacher" (*Journey* 121). The tragedy for Susie and for Cephas was that there were "no books, no little shrine to truth, no music teacher. In that small backwoods cabin crowded by poverty and isolation, there was no room for them" (121). Yet, as Smith finds in the next chapter when she meets another motel operator, Timothy, respite does not necessarily depend on being privileged enough to have access to books and music. Though Timothy too grew up in poverty, he is in every way the inverse of Cephas.[6] Unlike Cephas, Timothy had the luck of having a Good Teacher, despite the lack of resources. Miss Molly "taught five grades, did her own janitoring, stoked the stove—and told us the most wonderful stories a boy ever listened to," and in telling her students about different places, people, and times, "she brought them all into that unpainted schoolhouse and its walls stretched like rubber" (122). It only takes one other person whose imaginative and creative Mary impulse has free rein to nurture those impulses in others.

An examination of Susie reaps some insight into the experience of southern women, particularly creative southern women. If, like Susie, they wanted to exercise their Martha impulses, they might be allowed to do so as long as it facilitated capitalism. If they had creative Mary impulses, in a world fixated on consumption and political power, they had no place at all except the backyard and the mental hospital. At this time, as Gladney observes, "between the two feminist movements of the twentieth century" (xiv), when women had at best indirect power to amass consumer goods and little or no power to produce them, as well as little or no political power, it is not surprising that these cultural emphases would leave women feeling isolated and unfulfilled. Susie's story offers a cautionary tale of what happens to a "little aborted artist . . . torn from the placenta of human resources," but it is also a story of hope for the impulse itself. Susie's Mary impulse is "still trying to grow" despite having so little with which to nourish itself (*Journey* 139), and if other Susies encounter a Good Teacher or even *The Journey*, they will be fed.

Notes

1. For further discussion of Smith's omission from studies defining southern literature, see Will Brantley's chapter on Lillian Smith in *Feminine Sense in Southern Memoir*.

2. *Killers of the Dream* was originally published in 1949. Increased interest in this work after the rise of civil rights activism led to the book's reissue in 1961 with a new foreword and revisions to the final two chapters, "Man against the Human Being" and "The Chasm and the Bridge."

3. When her father's business collapsed in 1915, Smith's family moved to Clayton, Georgia, where her parents started the Laurel Falls Camp for Girls. Smith interrupted her education at Piedmont College and then at the Peabody Conservatory, where she studied music, to return to Clayton to help her parents run the camp. In 1922 Smith went to Huzhow, China, to teach music at a Methodist missionary school but once again left in 1925 to help run the camp as her father's health declined. She eventually purchased the camp from him and, when he died in 1930, both directed the camp and cared for her ailing mother.

4. Smith started her "little magazine" *Pseudopodia*—later renamed *North Georgia Review* and then *South Today*—in 1936 and stopped publication in 1945.

Totalitarian Political Ideology and Women in *The Journey* 107

5. As graciously noted by an anonymous reviewer of an early version of this argument, Smith felt that the press of current events demanded Martha-like service from all southern artists: "We often say to each other, we're wasting our creative lives fighting this monster, segregation. . . . It hurts us as writers and artists to have to always give so much of our lives to it. And people call it your mission in life, and it's ghastly! Who wants a mission?" ("Miss Smith of Georgia").

6. See Haddox for a fuller comparison of Cephas and Timothy.

Works Cited

Blackwell, Louise, and Frances Clay. *Lillian Smith*. Twayne Publishers, 1971.

Brantley, Will. *Feminine Sense in Southern Memoir: Smith, Glasgow, Welty, Hellman, Porter, and Hurston*. UP of Mississippi, 1993.

Brinkmeyer, Robert H., Jr. *The Fourth Ghost: White Southern Writers and European Fascism, 1930–1950*. Louisiana State UP, 2009.

Casement, Ann. *Carl Gustav Jung*. SAGE, 2001.

Dale, John, and Christian Smith. "Martha and Mary: A Story for Men or Women?" *The Furrow*, vol. 49, no. 11, 1998, pp. 628–34.

Gladney, Margaret Rose, ed. *How Am I to Be Heard? Letters of Lillian Smith*. U of North Carolina P, 1993.

Gladney, Margaret Rose. "Preface." Gladney, pp. xiii–xviii.

Haddox, Thomas F. "Lillian Smith, Cold War Intellectual." *Southern Literary Journal*, vol. 44, no. 2, 2012, pp. 51–68.

King James Version. Bible Gateway, 2019. BibleGateway.com, https://www.biblegateway.com/versions. Accessed February 10, 2019.

Loveland, Anne C. *Lillian Smith, a Southerner Confronting the South: A Biography*. Louisiana State UP, 1986.

"Miss Smith of Georgia." Interview. Joan Titus Collection. Walter J. Brown Media Archives. Hargrett Rare Book and Manuscript Library. MS3757-0181. https://kaltura.uga.edu/media/t/1_0z6uw261/31261611.

Segal, Robert A. *Theorizing about Myth*. U of Massachusetts P, 1999.

Smith, Lillian. *The Journey*. World Publishing, 1954.

Smith, Lillian. *Killers of the Dream*, rev. ed. W. W. Norton, 1961.

Smith, Lillian. Letter to Dan Wickenden, October 16, 1961. Gladney, pp. 285–87.

Smith, Lillian. Letter to Lawrence Kubie, October 10, 1957. Gladney, pp. 217–18.

Smith, Lillian. Letter to Lawrence Kubie, April 5, 1965. Gladney, pp. 319–20.

Smith, Lillian. Letter to Margaret Sullivan, December 9, 1965. Gladney, pp. 336–38.

Smith, Lillian. Letter to Rochelle Girson, March 5, 1962. Gladney, pp. 294–95.

CHAPTER 5

Reading *One Hour* in the Time of #MeToo

—Cameron Williams Crawford

Lillian Smith's *One Hour* (1959) is too often read for its social critique and not for its artistry. Its plot is certainly sensational. Narrated by David Landrum, a priest at All Saints Episcopal Church, the novel recalls the time of "the trouble" in his small southern town of Windsor Hills. Eight-year-old Susan Newell accuses Dr. Mark Channing, a well-respected scientist and close friend of David's, of attempted rape. The allegation spreads like wildfire, and David—convinced that Mark is innocent and Susan is nothing more than a manipulative nymphet, a little girl "starved for . . . affection [who] might settle in her fantasy life for something crude and perverse" (104–5)—traces for us its destructive ripple effect on the people in his community. For this reason, *One Hour* is commonly read as a critique of Cold War–era McCarthyism. Smith herself, in a letter to her friend George Sion, acknowledged the McCarthy-era influence on her writing, explaining that her novel "searches modern man's heart and mind, looks at the 'dangers' of democracy, knowing that it, too, has its terrible dangers, different from those of communism. . . . The danger of the mob dominating the few who are artists, intellectuals, priests; the danger of the eight-year-old mentality of the masses drowning the poetic vision, the scientific knowledge" (244). Smith here also alludes to her own experience with "the danger of the mob" regarding the backlash to her work, specifically *Killers of the Dream* and *Now Is the Time*, which was suppressed by the publisher and removed from some bookstores and subsequently led to Smith being essentially blacklisted by the media. Writing *One Hour* was thus a deeply personal experience for Smith. As Margaret Rose Gladney observes, through the novel, "Smith was, in effect, addressing her own questions about *how* she was to be heard and *why* her ideas about social change and human relationships were so strongly resisted" (165). Those questions remain to be addressed—as does the manner of Smith's complicated artistry in raising them.

One Hour especially deserves reassessment now, particularly in light of what Smith somewhat flippantly described as its "mere plot": the accusation of sexual assault against a child. *One Hour* was written decades before the #MeToo movement went viral and forced a global reckoning with the scope, impact, and entrenched systemic nature of sexual violence in our culture and beyond. While Smith certainly understood literature as a tool of social and political change and was highly attuned to issues of gender inequality in the South, some of her personal letters reveal that she sympathized with Channing; as noted earlier, she compared Susan's mentality to that of a mob, "drowning the poetic knowledge, the scientific vision" (letter to George Sion, 244). As a twenty-first-century reader and scholar well versed in the contemporary discourse of rape culture and victim blaming, I find Smith's stance troubling and therefore worthy of interrogation. Smith's use of rape as a narrative device is anything but "mere plot"; it is no doubt significant, highly charged, and the moment to confront this point has never been more urgent.

But how do we read *One Hour* today? Why is it necessary to reassess Smith's treatment of rape in the era of #MeToo? How do we place Smith's southern novel within the larger context of national and global discussions of gender and sexual violence? As I suggest, *One Hour* wrestles with the treatment of women and sexuality in the mid-twentieth century. In her thorough portrayal of repressed white supremacist southern society, Smith provides a glimpse into the plight of women whose society does not value their voices. While acknowledging that Smith seems not to have *intended* a critique of male dominance in *One Hour*, I assert that, nonetheless, the problems inherent in that dominance rise to the surface of her keenly rendered painting of society. Smith has been acknowledged as a political writer, even pigeonholed as one, but the fact is that her political critique is a manifestation of her artistic choices. Her still mostly unrecognized strategies of representation are what make her "mere plot" so alive in a contemporary context where sexual violence as a fact of life has been opened to public acknowledgment. Indeed, Smith is often at her most interesting when her aesthetic choices reveal those places where "mere plot" breaks down and we see Smith struggling with the implications of her critique. Smith's work arguably helps us better understand—and thereby disrupts—our current attitudes toward women, along with the deep-rooted systems that allow for sexual violence to persist. In this way, attending to Smith's artistic choices both uncovers the roots of her achievement and casts new light on our own twenty-first-century #MeToo cultural moment.

To reassess *One Hour* in the contemporary #MeToo context, of course, requires understanding the history and trajectory of the movement. Before the hashtag was popularized, Me Too was started in 2006 by the civil rights activist Tarana Burke as a means of advocating for young women of color who experienced sexual violence. In 2017, the campaign was co-opted when the allegations of sexual assault against the Hollywood film producer Harvey Weinstein went public. The actress Alyssa Milano tweeted in response to the Weinstein scandal, suggesting her followers reply "me too" if they had ever experienced sexual harassment or assault, and the hashtag quickly went viral. Since then, #MeToo has become a way for people to share their own experiences with sexual violence and create a sense of solidarity with other survivors. Sharing these experiences has proved especially empowering for many survivors, not just for the purpose of building solidarity. As Pam Antil, president of the League of Women in Government, writes in an open letter on the league's website, "While difficult to hear, the sharing of these stories has opened up a much needed [and] overdue dialogue about not only how widespread the problem, but also how much women's complaints, stories and experiences have been discounted, not believed and/or not investigated properly by private and public sector organizations across the country." #MeToo has made conspicuous how prevalent and insidious the problem of sexual violence is, not just in the United States but around the globe, and in so doing, the campaign has given voice to those who are often silenced by cultural and other systemic barriers. *Time* magazine addressed this very point when it named "the Silence Breakers" its 2017 Person of the Year, solidifying the movement's place in our national dialogue.

Among the Silence Breakers included on the magazine's cover were the celebrities Ashley Judd, one of the first to come forward against Weinstein, and Taylor Swift, who took a defiant courtroom stand against the Denver radio DJ who groped her and, after he was fired, sued her for millions of dollars in damages. Swift countersued for only one dollar and went on to testify, during which the DJ's lawyer asked her, "on the witness stand, whether she felt bad that she'd gotten him fired." She replied: "I'm not going to let you or your client make me feel in any way that this is my fault. . . . I'm being blamed for the unfortunate events of his life that are a product of his decisions. Not mine" (Zacharek et al.). Also included were Susan Fowler, an engineer for Uber; Adama Iwu, a corporate lobbyist; and Isabel Pascual, a Mexican farmworker who used a pseudonym to protect her family (Zacharek et al.). In featuring this diverse group of women on the cover, *Time* recognized the important fact that white celebrity spokespeople are not the only ones whose experiences with sexual violence matter. And women have not been the only ones to say "#MeToo"; men, trans, and nonbinary folks have also added to the conversation, reminding us how necessary it is to keep the movement intersectional and how desperately we need to listen to those underrepresented voices that so often get sidelined or drowned out by those of heteronormative, cisgender white women.

#MeToo continues to spread awareness about the scale of sexual violence around the world, revealing how deeply entrenched are the structures that allow for its persistence.

In addition to revealing the scale of sexual harassment and assault, #MeToo has compelled us to confront the scope. Many #MeToo stories have provoked vital discussion (and debate) about the definition of consent and what constitutes assault, forcing us to examine some of the murkier areas of this complex issue. As Julianne Escobedo Shepherd writes in an article for *Jezebel*, "#MeToo's next direction is toward a deeper look at some of the most common and harder-to-define experiences. It's looking toward a more equitable world in which women and other marginalized genders can live less fearfully, by digging deeper into the gray areas and educating all of us about the harm they perpetuate." These gray areas include harmful or toxic behavior that is "inequitable but isn't illegal," like manipulation and coercion, "the messy contours" that are "far more nuanced and more difficult to trace than behaviors that violate the law." The allegation brought forth against the actor and comedian Aziz Ansari is one such case involving messy, gray-area behavior. In 2018, babe.net published a story about "Grace," a Brooklyn photographer whose name was changed to protect her identity, who describes a date with Ansari "that turned into the worst night of my life" (Way). According to Grace, the evening started out pleasantly enough but quickly took an uncomfortable turn when, at dinner, Ansari suddenly became "very eager for them to leave." The two went back to Ansari's apartment, where he continued to rush things with Grace, making continual sexual advances toward her despite her admonition "Whoa, let's relax for a sec. Let's chill." Though Grace engaged in sexual activity with Ansari, she claims "she used verbal and non-verbal cues to indicate how uncomfortable and distressed she was," but Ansari persisted. The evening concluded after Grace performed oral sex on Ansari, not because she particularly wanted to, but because, she says, "I think I just felt really pressured. It was literally the most unexpected thing I thought would happen at that moment because I told him I was uncomfortable."

It is perhaps this part of Grace's story that has sparked the most reaction, much of it contentious. While some saw Ansari's behavior as aggressive and entitled, others found the fault with Grace, blaming her for encouraging Ansari's advances and wondering why she didn't simply leave the moment she felt uncomfortable. However, as several critics have rightfully remarked, the decision to leave is not always so simple. As Caroline Framke notes, the discussion surrounding Grace's account "has become a flashpoint of conflicting, interwoven opinions, painting a complex portrait of the power and limitations of the #MeToo movement," yet "the reactions to the report are more telling than the report itself" ("The Controversy"). Both the story and the public discourse surrounding it reveal "our broken attitudes toward sex." Anna North writes:

> What [Grace] describes—a man repeatedly pushing sex without noticing (or without caring about) what she wants—is something many, many women have experienced in encounters with men. And while few men have committed the litany of misdeeds of which Weinstein has been accused, countless men have likely behaved as Grace says Ansari did—focusing on their own desires without recognizing what their partner wants. It is the sheer commonness of Grace's experience that makes it so important to talk about.

Grace's experience with Ansari is a difficult one to grapple with precisely because of its "sheer commonness." So many women have had similar encounters with men that left them feeling rattled, uncomfortable, or violated in some way, yet those experiences are not so easy to label as "assault" or "harassment." This is but one example of how the #MeToo movement has forced a reckoning with the scope of sexual violence by asking us to assess those messy gray areas that continue to be problematic.

Although #MeToo has produced some encouraging results, it has not been without backlash, as the case with Grace and Ansari makes evident. Parul Seghal calls the movement one "full of reappraisals—of beloved artists, public figures, ourselves." Indeed, stories like Grace's that have emerged as part of #MeToo have encouraged people to reevaluate or talk to others about some of their own past experiences, which, for many survivors, "has been very helpful . . . in terms of the validation" (Jagannathan). As Framke writes, "Women are speaking out about sexual misconduct, more publicly and in greater numbers than before—and, more than before, they are being heard" ("The Aziz Ansari Story"). Many people, however, feel threatened by or afraid of this movement of reappraisals. In a scathing critique of Grace's allegations against Ansari, Caitlin Flanagan of *The Atlantic* blames #MeToo for making women "angry, temporarily powerful—and very, very dangerous." Others similarly think #MeToo has devolved into a pretext for women with an ax to grind to mercilessly seek "punishment for every kind of male sexual misconduct, from the grotesque to the disappointing" (Flanagan). Some have even gone so far as to label #MeToo a "witch hunt."

The term "witch hunt" became the rallying cry for critics of the movement in the 2018 case of Dr. Christine Blasey Ford's allegation of sexual assault against Supreme Court nominee Brett Kavanaugh. After Kavanaugh's nomination to the highest court in the country, Ford sent a confidential letter to Senator Dianne Feinstein, in which Ford accused Kavanaugh of assaulting her, physically and sexually, while the two were in high school in the 1980s. Feinstein later gave the letter to Senator Chuck Grassley, explicitly instructing him to keep the information private. Grassley, however, released the letter to the public, and Ford was subsequently called to testify against Kavanaugh in front of the Senate Judiciary Committee (Hayes). The case played out, as Rebecca Solnit points out in an essay for *The Guardian*, in a way that was all too familiar. Kavanaugh denied the accusation, and Ford's character and credibility were brought under fire. Like so many other women who have spoken up about sexual abuse, Ford was "discredited, shamed, blamed, and disbelieved" by Kavanaugh's supporters (Solnit). The Republican National Committee claimed that the true victim was Kavanaugh, writing in an email "soliciting signatures for a petition in support of the judge" that the hearing was nothing short of "a televised witch hunt playing out in front of his own family. . . . Democrats only want to smear this man because he was nominated by President Trump" (Lim). Moreover, some who supported Kavanaugh worked to smear the "feminists" who protested in defense of Ford, recasting them as an angry mob, "swarming the Capitol steps" and "clawing at the doors of the Supreme Court" (Robbins).

Almost sixty years may separate the Kavanaugh hearing and *One Hour*, but Smith's novel evokes the language of the witch hunt, "the danger of the mob" that turns against Channing (and others) after Susan's allegation. In fact, the rhetoric of #MeToo reverberates throughout Smith's novel, most pointedly through the first-person narrator, David Landrum. Privileging a white, male perspective is one of the foremost literary strategies Smith employs as a way of exploring issues of gender and sexual violence, and David—the authoritative, masculine voice that controls the overarching narrative—is a prime example of this. David is an Episcopal priest at All Saints Church, and in recalling the events surrounding Susan's accusation, he reveals as much about his southern community's system of gender and sexual politics as he does about his own personal attitudes toward women. The conversations he recounts with his friend Neel—a doctor of clinical psychology who is a "special assistant to the police chief of the city and is in charge of the Juvenile Bureau" (7)—provide some of the sharpest insights into how toxic misogyny permeates the Windsor Hills community at the most structural levels. At the outset of his narrative, Neel tells David about "a puzzling situation" involving some of David's parishioners (8). Neel tells David that when he responded to the report of an attempted rape (making a point to say that Susan's mother, Renie, used that word), he "found a distraught woman and a calm, slightly resentful little girl who obviously wanted the story told in a certain way. She corrected her mother a number of times. The child looked all right except for a scratch on her arm. The arm was bandaged" (8). Neel also describes Susan as a "cool little number. Or extremely scared. I'm not sure which. She has a face that looks four years old one moment, twelve the next" (9). Immediately Neel raises doubts about the "situation" and directs his skepticism at the women accusers, Susan and her mother, not at the man they accuse. David conveys this conversation to us, shaping the narrative and thus our perception of Susan and Renie. Placing David—a white male, it bears repeating, whose occupation as priest marks him as a moral authority figure—in the role of narrator is an artistic choice that Smith uses to explore issues of gender and power.

David is the novel's primary authoritative masculine voice, but the aforementioned example also speaks to the ways that Smith's literary strategy is complexly layered, as David's narrative privileges other authoritative, masculine perspectives, like Neel's. Neel works with the police force, the pinnacle of municipal authority. Through conversations with Neel, David's first-person narrative reveals the ways in which gender roles are defined in Windsor Hills and shows us that men are the ones with the most power. David's conversations with Neel also reveal that part of the reason for Neel's reluctance to believe Susan derives from an intense, deep-seated hostility toward women stemming from his relationship with his sister. During a conversation about Susan's accusation, David mentions Renie and a traumatic experience she endured when she was young. Neel interrupts to call Renie "a bitch from way back"; he then tells David how he knows "her kind" because he has "a sister just like her," Hattie Belle, who since the age of ten has "been layin out of nights . . . with any man she can cheat" (106). Because of Hattie Belle, Neel admits he has struggled to stay objective about Susan's case. Yet he goes on to deliver the following diatribe:

> I don't know what makes a woman a bitch. I've read hundreds of books on psychology, delinquency, crime, broken homes, all the rest of it. I've never found out. The theories won't stick to Hattie Belle. She slides right out of them. They won't fit [Renie], either. You can say it is something they feel about their body. It is, but it's a lot more than

that. They use it like a lethal weapon, sure; and without scruple. They take care, too, because it's their bank account and insurance policy. But there's something else: they're addicted to men. And they hate them the same way an alcoholic hates his whisky; loathes it and yet must have it. I say this and yet I know it is not right, either. Not quite. When Hattie Belle was no more than two or three she was already at it, standing by the side of the road holding her dress up and no pants on. That kind of thing. Laughing, daring them to look, saying, *Give me a penny*. But—now this is the point: anybody who didn't give her a penny, paid for it; and anybody who did, paid, too. She'd run tell pappy on all of them. (106–7; italics in original)

We can find a lot to unpack in Neel's invective, primarily as it illuminates his earlier comment about Susan looking four years old one minute and twelve the next; it reveals the ways our culture sexualizes women essentially from birth and then punishes them for being sexual. It furthermore demonstrates how women are regularly portrayed as manipulative seductresses, an image still very much in circulation today. As Solnit reminds us in her piece about the Kavanaugh hearing, "We know that women have been portrayed, ever since Eve offered Adam an apple, as temptresses, more responsible for men's act than men themselves are, and that various religions still inculcate this view, and in recent time various judges and journalists have acceded to it, even blaming female children for 'seducing' their adult abuser." Through Neel, *One Hour* confronts the same harmful assumptions that linger in the #MeToo twenty-first century. David-as-narrator privileging Neel's voice in this way is an artistic means through which Smith confronts the gender politics of her time and place.

David's shaping of the overarching story—interpreting and forwarding meaning—is a continuation of Smith's narrative strategy. Even as he observes and is concerned by Neel's misogyny, David follows his example, letting his own personal opinions and ideas about gender color how he receives the information about Susan's accusation. When David realizes who Neel is describing—"*Susan*"—

Reading *One Hour* in the Time of #MeToo

he identifies her as the only child "who sat with her parents in the fourth pew on the right and had been carrying on a cold war with my sermons since I came here, trying to divert me with her antics" (9; italics in original). Exactly what Susan's antics are remains unclear. This comment, however, illustrates how David's first impulse is to disbelieve Susan's story, then to call her character into question. The portrait David paints of Susan is not a flattering one; he depicts her as difficult—"her antics"—and duplicitous, referring to her on multiple occasions as "the brat." David continues to disbelieve, discredit, and defame Susan throughout his narrative. "Little girls make up these things, one often reads," he says to Neel, suggesting, of course, that Susan is lying (10).

Later, in a similar example, David has a conversation with Susan when he catches her sneaking into his rectory. During this conversation, Susan tells David about her imaginary friend, Boody, who was hurt by "a bad man." The story matches Susan's alleged experience with Channing; in fact, Susan slips and inserts herself into this story more than once. In one instance, she says, "I got lots of presents because a bad man hurt me." David replies, "You were not hurt. . . . I see it in your eyes. You're making it up" (92–93). It is imperative to note how Susan behaves during this conversation, notably as it is David who *tells* us how Susan behaves. She wavers back and forth regarding some details of the night in question. To David, this is a telltale sign that Susan is being untruthful. However, such lapses in memory are not at all unusual for survivors of trauma like sexual assault. One of the many important discussions #MeToo has prompted—especially surrounding cases like Grace/Ansari and Ford/Kavanaugh—is about how traumatic memory works. According to Brian Resnick, "Often after traumatic incidents, some parts are dwelled on and can even get exaggerated over time, while other parts become muddied. But the central event can be recalled with accuracy." The details change, but the central event of Susan's story stays the same. David keeps questioning her, however, telling her she is lying, to the point where he writes a confession for her on a slip of paper and asks her to sign it; it reads,

"There wasn't anybody in the store but me. The cat scratched me. That is all. Yours truly—" (97). After Susan leaves, he looks at it and sees that Susan has signed it, but she has added a significant postscript: *"P.S. I was joking. He did hurt me too, that bad man. Susan"* (98; italics in original). The scene is an uncomfortable one, especially now, if we consider the power dynamics from a twenty-first-century perspective. Susan is eight years old, and David is an older, male authority figure who repeatedly tells her he thinks she is making her story up and then pressures her into signing a "confession." His behavior is inappropriate at best and coercive at worst, and it is yet another example of how David controls the novel's overarching narrative.

Another part of this narrative strategy is to cast key women as "bitches," namely, Renie. The irony of the aforementioned scene is that David believes it is Renie who has been coercive, having persuaded Susan into accusing Channing of sexual assault. As David tells Neel, Renie endured her own traumatic experience when she was younger, "fourteen, she thinks, or fifteen or sixteen, she is not sure" (28). David recalls Renie's account of the incident:

> I went out to cut the okra—I was cutting the pods and humming and then suddenly, between the big leaves I saw two black hands. I screamed and dropped the pan—and at that moment, I saw his face and recognized him. He was laughing good-naturedly and I wanted to laugh too, I remember that: I wanted to laugh and say, You sort of scared me. But I kept on screaming and ran in and out between the rows of okra and the running scared me even more and he ran after me, I heard him behind me, I think I did. But when I looked he wasn't there any more. I knew his name, I had seen him on the place all my life. (28–29)

The experience haunts Renie into adulthood, and because of it, according to David, Renie has "a phobia about rape" (105). David assumes that Renie's phobia is a result of a near-rape experience at the hands of a black man; yet, on closer examination, it seems that

Reading *One Hour* in the Time of #MeToo

Renie is most traumatized by the aftermath of the incident, when she told her father about the boy who chased her. Despite her insistence that she "was just scared," her father whipped the boy mercilessly in front of her. Renie, "unable to bear the sight of his eyes and the sounds of his screams and the lashing, ran into her room and lay across the bed with a pillow over her head" (29). Years later, Renie believes she sees the boy—a man now—and, according to David, is afraid he will find her and hurt (read: rape) her. David sees this as part of a pattern of Renie's behavior, and he points to this experience as evidence of Renie falsely accusing Channing of assaulting Susan. In other words, David uses this past experience against her, to characterize her as "hysterical," confused, and thereby as a reason to discredit her.

Although many critics think Smith avoids any meaningful discussion of race in *One Hour*, in this episode, the fact that the boy is black is crucial. It is through Renie's experience that Smith offers a sharp commentary on the insidiousness of "the southern rape complex," a term coined by W. J. Cash in the early 1940s to describe whites' fear of the sexual violation of a white woman by an aggressive black man. Smith herself explains this complex as a "poisonous idea" in *Killers of the Dream*, where she explores the origins of the "race-sex-sin spiral" (117, 121). Writing about "the back-yard temptation"—a reference to antebellum slaveholding practices in which enslaved people of color "were brought into our back yards and left there for generations" (117)—as a means for white men to justify the sexual exploitation of black women, Smith asserts, "The white man's roles as slaveholder and Christian and puritan were exacting far more than the strength of his mind could sustain.... The more trails the white man made to his back-yard cabins, the higher he raised his white wife on her pedestal, the less he enjoyed her whom he had put there, for statues after all are only nice things to look at" (121). The more the white man's "guilt, shame, fear, lust spiraled each other," the more he became suspicious of his white women and projected these feelings onto black men. "And when he did that," observes Smith, "a madness seized our people" (121). Out of that madness emerged the southern rape complex. This racialized discourse of rape forms the very foundation of modern southern culture. As Diane Roberts explains in her seminal study of southern womanhood, "The Civil War and Reconstruction were inscribed as a violent descent from grace: the land was 'raped'; 'Paradise,' built by the slave economy, was lost. If the land lost its innocence, its walking symbol, the southern woman, was in danger of losing hers" (103–4).

Gender roles in the South are thus constructed on this same mythology; Katie Snyder, the daughter of David's friend Dewey—the warden of All Saints—observes as much in *One Hour*. Recounting how her father told her about Channing allegedly following Susan after school, Katie remarks, "It was kind of a throw-back to age six. Because Mother, even as sensible as she was about things, would warn me when I was little to be careful and never speak to a strange man, never let myself be left alone with one, with even the men I knew, in lonely places—" before suggesting, "It must do something to little females to be warned from the time they can walk, against men" (122–23). Here Smith elaborates her concern with the dangers of repressed sexuality, misogyny, and racism in a "patriarchal-puritanic system which psychically castrated its women, who in turn psychically castrated their children, male and female, by the burden of anxiety they laid on their minds" (*Killers* 118). It *does* do something, to both women and men; as Smith argues, the "race-sex-sin" spiral is steeped in "*Southern tradition, segregation*" and has "soaked up the fears of our people; little private fantasies of childhood have crept there for hiding, unacknowledged arsenals of hate have been stored there, and a loyalty covering up a lack of self-criticism has glazed the words over with sanctity. No wonder the saying of them aloud can stir anxieties until there are times when it seems we have lost our grasp on reality" (154–55; italics in original). Yet complicating Smith's diagnosis of the problem is *One Hour*'s ambiguity regarding Channing's guilt, anticipating #MeToo's revelation that misogynistic attitudes, behaviors, and gender expectations are not just regional but national, even global. Katie, Renie, and Susan—their fear of being assaulted, their recognition of men's violent potential, does not exist in a vacuum. Claud reveals to David that Renie's father continually raped the young black women on their plantation (the "back-yard temptation"). The real possibility of being raped is therefore something southern white women absorbed from their culture. Hence their perceptions and behavior must walk a tightrope between the irrational fear of black men's sexuality and a reasonable sense of self-preservation in a society that robs them of the power to judge and label their own experiences. Regardless of Smith's intentions, her artistic decisions in composing *One Hour* make visible the insidious prevalence, the deeply entrenched nature of sexual violence in the South and beyond.

Therefore, in addition to exploring the "mob mentality" that the Cold War fostered, Smith confronts and critiques, as well, the notion developed by second-wave feminists in the 1970s: the existence of rape culture. As Amber J. Keyser explains, this concept "makes excuses for male sexual violence and pretends that assault and rape are normal and inevitable" (12). The culture that Keyser defines, drawing also on the work of Emilie Buchwald, Pamela R. Fletcher, and Martha Roth, may as well be that of *One Hour*. "In a rape culture," Keyser says, as if she were discussing the situation of Susan and Renie, "women perceive a continuum of threatened violence that ranges from sexual remarks to sexual touching to rape itself. A rape culture condones physical and emotional terrorism against women and presents it as the norm" (12–13). As *One Hour* brilliantly portrays, the variables that contribute to the proliferation of rape culture—including dismissing or discrediting women's lived experiences—are rooted in patriarchal systems that place men as superior and in positions of power and women as inferior and that value men's voices as authoritative.

Smith's choice of a male narrator recognizes this fact. David's first-person narrative dramatizes the ways in which gender roles are defined in Windsor Hills and shows, even if unconsciously, that men inevitably assume the power to frame and tell women's stories. In Smith's narrative, men control and disseminate the information regarding women's bodies. David learns of Susan's accusation against Channing from his friend Neel; when David discusses Susan's case, he does so primarily with other men who are also in positions of power. In addition to Neel, he goes to Dr. Guthrie to discuss Susan's case. Dr. Guthrie explains to David that he examined Susan after the incident and found no evidence that Susan had been sexually assaulted, only scratched on her arm. And David defers to Dr. Guthrie, placing more value on his (male) expertise than on Susan's testimony of her own experience. Smith makes us feel the disturbing, even creepy, implications of this older, male doctor examining eight-year-old Susan, who has just claimed to have been sexually assaulted by an older man. It is as if the doctor has been licensed by the state to replicate the assault—to sanitize it in the name of "helping" the girl. As we now know, survivors frequently relive the trauma of their sexual assault during a medical examination. Smith portrays the silence of this encounter—how Susan does not or cannot speak—through David's need to discuss the incident with Claud, who, as the Newells' paterfamilias, is apparently a more reliable source than either Renie or Susan. As Smith portrays the exchange through the hapless David, Claud literally steals Susan's story as his own. Snidely, he suggests that the only reason Renie reported the incident was to get back at him for being unfaithful to her. He has turned attention away from the victim to himself and, correctly, trusts David's instinct to sanitize what has happened. *One Hour* repeatedly makes visible how rape culture is perpetuated when men's voices are given more power than women's, and we see this through David—the priest, the supposed symbol of morality and honesty who controls the entire narrative—when he lies to protect Channing, claiming to have seen him at home at a time when Channing actually was out. Moreover, when David learns what Channing was really doing in the store—something inappropriate at the latrine—he excuses it as typical but harmless male behavior. In Windsor Hills, this system of men protecting men, claiming absolute authority and power, erases women's voices from the equation and thus contributes to the perpetuation of rape culture.

Just as readers have not always recognized the dexterity and complexity of Smith's artistry, so we have perhaps not been able to see until now how *One Hour* makes legible the story of #MeToo. Its narrative pulse points are vitally concerned with the same questions and concerns about gender, sexuality, and structures of power that have been prompted by this global movement. By presenting us with David as first-person narrator, Smith examines the ways women's voices are silenced, their lived experiences denied by patriarchal systems. *One Hour* is therefore important in the twenty-first century, as it can illuminate our own attitudes toward women, can help us to recognize those facets of our culture that allow for sexual violence to persist. Only when we recognize the issue can we work to dismantle it, and through her deft employment of literary strategies, Smith shines a light on it.

Works Cited

Antil, Pam. "Why Sharing YOUR #MeToo and #IWillSpeakUp Stories Is Important in #LocalGov." League of Women in Government, November 30, 2017, https://www.leagueofwomeningovernment.org/2017/11/sharing-metoo-iwill speakup-stories-important-localgov.

Flanagan, Caitlin. "The Humiliation of Aziz Ansari." *The Atlantic*, January 14, 2018, https://www.theatlantic.com/entertainment/archive/2018/01/the-humili ation-of-aziz-ansari/550541.

Framke, Caroline. "The Controversy around Babe.net's Aziz Ansari Story, Explained." *Vox*, January 18, 2018, https://www.vox.com/culture/2018/1/17/ 16897440/aziz-ansari-allegations-babe-me-too.

Garcia, Sandra E. "The Woman Who Created #MeToo Long before Hashtags." *New York Times*, October 20, 2017, https://www.nytimes.com/2017/10/20/us/ me-too-movement-tarana-burke.html.

Gladney, Margaret Rose, ed. *How Am I to Be Heard? Letters of Lillian Smith*. U of North Carolina P, 1993.

Haddox, Thomas F. "Lillian Smith, Cold War Intellectual." *Southern Literary Journal*, vol. 44, no. 2, Spring 2012, pp. 51–68.

Hayes, Christal. "Read Christine Blasey Ford's Letter Detailing the Alleged Assault by Brett Kavanaugh." *USA Today*, September 23, 2018, https://www.usatoday .com/story/news/politics/2018/09/23/christine-blasey-ford-letter-alleged -assault-brett-kavanaugh/1406932002.

Jagannathan, Meera. "This Is How #MeToo Is Impacting Sexual Assault Survivors' Mental Health." *MarketWatch*, October 1, 2018, https://www.marketwatch.com/story/this-is-how-metoo-is-impacting-sexual-assault-survivors-mental-health-2018-10-01.

Keyser, Amber J. *No More Excuses: Dismantling Rape Culture*. Twenty-First Century Books, 2019.

Lim, Naomi. "RNC Calls Kavanaugh Accusations a 'Witch Hunt.'" *Washington Examiner*, September 26, 2018, https://www.washingtonexaminer.com/news/rnc-calls-kavanaugh-accusations-a-witch-hunt.

North, Anna. "The Aziz Ansari Story Is Ordinary. That's Why We Have to Talk about It." *Vox*, January 16, 2018, https://www.vox.com/identities/2018/1/16/16894722/aziz-ansari-grace-babe-me-too.

Resnick, Brian. "Donald Trump's Attack on Christine Blasey Ford's Memory Is Cruel—and Wrong." *Vox*, October 3, 2018, https://www.vox.com/science-and-health/2018/9/20/17879768/brett-kavanaugh-christine-blasey-ford-trump-memory-psychology.

Robbins, James S. "Trump-Era Protests, Kavanaugh Drama Show We Need Less Democracy." *USA Today*, October 9, 2018, https://www.usatoday.com/story/opinion/2018/10/09/brett-kavanaugh-protestors-supreme-court-liberal-mob-democracy-constitution-column/1564490002.

Seghal, Parul. "#MeToo Is All Too Real. But to Better Understand It, Turn to Fiction." *New York Times*, May 1, 2019, https://www.nytimes.com/2019/05/01/books/novels-me-too-movement.html.

Shepherd, Julianne Escobedo. "The Next Step for #MeToo Is into the Gray Areas." *Jezebel*, September 24, 2018, https://jezebel.com/the-next-step-for-metoo-is-into-the-gray-areas-1829269384.

Smith, Lillian. *Killers of the Dream*. 1949. W. W. Norton, 1994.

Smith, Lillian. Letter to George Sion. *How Am I to Be Heard? Letters of Lillian Smith*, edited by Margaret Rose Gladney, U of North Carolina P, 1993, pp. 243–45.

Smith, Lillian. *One Hour*. 1959. U of North Carolina P, 1994.

Solnit, Rebecca. "The Brett Kavanaugh Case Shows We Still Blame Women for the Sins of Men." *The Guardian*, September 21, 2018, https://www.theguardian.com/commentisfree/2018/sep/21/brett-kavanaugh-blame-women-anita-hill-cosby-weinstein.

Way, Katie. "I Went on a Date with Aziz Ansari. It Turned into the Worst Night of My Life." babe.net, January 13, 2018, https://babe.net/2018/01/13/aziz-ansari-28355.

Zacharek, Stephanie, et al. "The Silence Breakers." *Time*, 2017, https://time.com/time-person-of-the-year-2017-silence-breakers.

CHAPTER 6

Positive Self-Identity: Neighborliness in Lillian Smith's *Memory of a Large Christmas*

—April Conley Kilinski

Lillian Smith's 1962 memoir *Memory of a Large Christmas*, which originally appeared as a shorter piece in *Life* magazine in 1961, recalls her life as one of nine children growing up in a close-knit southern family. The family operates by a clear set of values and thrives through agrarian practices, intergenerational family dynamics, and faith. Throughout the narrative, Smith's parents (and particularly her father) reinforce these values through scripture recitation, large family meals comprising farm-sourced foods, gift giving, and, most importantly, hospitality. Smith specifically focuses her discussion of these aspects of her family life in her recounting of the family's rituals around the holiday season.

Smith's tone throughout the narrative captures the dynamics of her family during the Christmas season with wit and humor, and indeed, many reviewers of the book use words like "delightful," "funny," and "charming" to describe it. Smith's own description of the book to her friend Marvin Rich in a letter dated December 1, 1961, affirms these descriptions: "I've done a piece about Christmas in our big family in the first decade of the century. It is warm and sort of quaint and amusing. I did a very long piece but it had to be cut for *Life* . . . so some of the wackiest scenes are out; [but] . . . I live in a small town: and *these* people would get all the fun and wackiness in the piece and thoroughly enjoy it" (291). Indeed, the longer version published by Norton in the spring of 1962 while Smith underwent cobalt treatments for lung cancer includes several "wacky, absurd and wonderful scenes" that endear her family and their way of life to the reader (letter to Marvin Rich 291).

One should not overlook, however, the various aspects of conflict, disruption, and even pain inherent in the events of the text. In the opening pages of the narrative, for example, Smith notes that even in the expansiveness of her childhood home—which boasts room for extended family as well as pets while still leaving room for quiet corners to contemplate and enjoy being alone—Big Grandma is an unsettling and unwelcome visitor. Big Grandma comes to participate in the hog killing, an arguably traumatic event in the text. Additionally, toward the end of the memoir, the family's economic downturn necessitates a move to Georgia, where the family experiences poverty. And in the face of that poverty, a chain gang of forty-eight prisoners (many of whom have committed violent crimes) comes to the family's house for Christmas dinner.

In fact, considering *Memory of a Large Christmas* in the context of her other autobiographical writings such as *Killers of the Dream* (1949) and *The Journey* (1954), Smith recognized that a book such as this might seem disingenuous. In the letter to Marvin Rich mentioned earlier, she notes that "there is an odd kind of truth in the juxtaposition of this merry, gay memory of Christmas to my *Killers of the Dream*. People will say, But how can both be true? That is the magic and wonder and horror of life: that both can be true, and are" (291). The notion that juxtaposition helped to reveal the truth carries over as a theme in several of Smith's other letters from around this time.

In a letter to Bertha Barnett dated April 6, 1962, Smith notes that "the wise things come to us from a deeper part of our nature than the reason, this I know; whether from mythic mind or from the transcendent spirit or from both, I cannot know—most likely from both. I know faith is not something one wills but something that comes,

Neighborliness in *Memory of a Large Christmas* 129

like happiness when one loves deeply and is concerned deeply with others" (296). The love and concern for others Smith describes here resounds in the happiness that she captures in the text of *Memory of a Large Christmas*, happiness shaped by genuine acts of compassion, kindness, and generosity to others throughout the text.

More importantly, Smith's text reveals that the happiness there moves beyond the dualism of juxtaposing this memoir with her other autobiographical writings. As the foregoing quotation reveals, the truth is a matter not just of either/or but of both/and. Indeed, in a letter to Alice Shoemaker dated October 30, 1965, Smith writes, "I know that dualism is wrong; there is no clear evil and no clear good, no clear black and no clear white; it is wrapped together in a terrible tangle; and it is our duty—I think it is God's purpose!—for us to have to unwrap it, learning more about the good because of the evil meshed with it" (329). Significantly, Smith wrote *Memory of a Large Christmas* after most of her other writings, and as she explains in a letter to Maxwell Geismar dated January 1961,

> A curious thing about *Strange Fruit* is that it proved, for me, to be therapy that removed a long amnesia about my hometown. I was born and reared in "Maxwell, Georgia." At the age of seventeen I left there.... So then, ten years later, on a trip to Florida, I went back to that little town. When I arrived, I was a complete stranger.... Ten years later, I began to write *Strange Fruit*. I worked on it six years and when I completed it my memory of ten thousand, maybe ten million details, had returned. (214–15)

Notably writing in the same year that *Memory of a Large Christmas* appeared in *Life* magazine, Smith recalls how writing about the "evils" of the South also helped her to recover her memories and connection to her home, allowing her to assert four years later that "dualism is wrong." Having recovered these memories and understanding that one gains a fuller sense of the world and the self by seeing the "good because of the evil meshed with it," Smith includes not only the "wacky" and humorous memories of her childhood Christmases but also elements of pain and uncertainty—aspects of her childhood and early adulthood that caused lasting wounds.

Rather than undermine the positive aspects of the memories in the rest of the text, however, these disruptions and conflicts, mediated through intersubjective creativity and relationships, create a more positive sense of self for Smith as she looks back on her life and recalls the numerous acts of "neighborliness" that her family extends to those around them. I use the term "neighborliness" in the sense that Jenny Edkins uses it in her essay "Time, Personhood, Politics." There she argues that "neighbourliness is an interaction based on acknowledgement of finitude, and of what is missing— an acknowledgement of the impossibility of completeness and a recognition of the trauma around which each person constitutes a fantasy of subjectivity" (138). When Smith's family acknowledges the finitude and the impossibility of completeness in those around them, Smith does not step out of the fantasy of subjectivity; instead she gains a better understanding of her subjectivity in *relation* to others. Drawing primarily on the Lacanian psychoanalytic theory of Jenny Edkins and Jessica Benjamin, I will argue that these conflicted interactions allow Smith to enter what Benjamin characterizes as a "transformational space of thirdness," a moral space that moves past blame to a space of healing.

In *Beyond Doer and Done To: Recognition Theory, Intersubjectivity and the Third*, Jessica Benjamin asserts that "the position of 'the Third' . . . is the position in which we implicitly recognize the other as a 'like subject,' a being we can experience as an 'other mind.' The Third refers to a position constituted through holding the tension of recognition between difference and sameness, taking the other to be a separate but equivalent center of initiative and with whom nonetheless feelings and intentions can be shared" (4). The notion of sharing, for Benjamin, begins in the preverbal stage between mothers and infants and extends into healthy relationships when individuals can give and receive recognition by aligning intentions or resonating feeling by "paradoxically . . . tolerating the inevitable interactive shifts from alignment to misalignment and back" (4).

Benjamin acknowledges the precarious nature of this process, as well as the tendency for relationships to collapse into "twoness, a relational formation in which the other appears as object or objectifying, unresponsive or injuring, threatening to erase one's own subjectivity or be oneself erased. This relational formation, based on splitting, takes shape as the complementarity of doer and done to, but there are many other permutations: accuser and accused, helpless and coercive, even victim and perpetrator" (4). Recalling Lillian Smith's own words about dualism quoted earlier, the dangers inherent in "twoness" in Benjamin's configuration reduce human interaction to what Buber calls an "I and it," rather than an "I and thou," configuration (qtd. in Benjamin 10). As Benjamin notes, "In short, the question is whether doing is *with* or *to*: doing *to* me implies that complementary twoness of opposing doer and done to, while doing *with* suggests that shared state of fitting in, coordination, or purposeful negotiation of difference that will be called thirdness" (5). By reading Smith's narrative against her other writings, one can apply Benjamin's clinical ideas in a textual context to show how Smith engages with her memories and her family through an *intersubjective* lens to achieve this space of purposeful negotiation of difference in her memoir. In so doing, she also gains a more positive sense of her own self and of humanity.

As Benjamin notes, "The argument for finding oneself by going into the not-self and returning to a now different and altered self (marked by the alterity it has encountered) points toward the underlying movement of intersubjectivity. To realize this transformation not primarily as a loss but rather as enrichment of self requires the movement between self and not-self that mirrors the more universal movement between oneness and thirdness" (12). In fact, Smith knew that understanding herself in light of others represented a way to understand the human experience when she said at the end of *The Journey* that "if we can in our imagination go back to that primal moment . . . of the separation which takes place between mother and child; . . . we can accept and understand it as a prototype of all human ordeal" (207). By exploring her own childhood memories—here the happy ones—and placing them in an intersubjective context of "the Third," Smith once again seeks to enter the more human experience that calls for relationship and healing.

After beginning her narrative by describing the expansiveness of her childhood home, Smith notes that "it was only when Big Grandma came that we began to scramble for hide-outs, for Big Grandma filled up the whole place. She could scrounge even Christmas" (12). Smith's mother reminds the children that Big Grandma comes because of her skill with the hog killing, and nobody can make sausage like their grandmother. They all love her sausage. Smith writes, "Yes we did. But we didn't love Big Grandma. Especially at Christmas" (13). Later we learn that Big Grandma is called such because "not only was she wide, she had a habit of reaching over to your plate with her fork when both your hands were busy and spearing the morsel you had saved for last" (15–16). Thus we understand that her "scrounging" and "filling" up the house come from her size and her propensity to steal food.

However, even these traits are redeemed for good when Smith recounts the way the children took turns rebelling against her father's injunction to recite scripture every morning before breakfast. She tells of one particularly well executed rebellion when her fifteen-year-old brother orchestrates all the children in a recitation of the Song of Solomon, and she also recounts how her eleven-year-old sister rebelled by performing a genealogy in Genesis. When her father scolds her, it is Big Grandma who comes to her defense; Big Grandma also offers her some sausage and tells her to eat because "eating would make everything all right" (18). While this advice includes clear inherent issues for our twenty-first-century ears (one should not drown one's problems with food, etc.), Smith redeems her grandmother here by recognizing her desire to help her granddaughter, as well as her willingness to give of herself in the form of her best food (the sausage she helped to make). Moreover, Big Grandma gives the only advice she knows how to give: to eat when one feels sad. While problematic, it

Neighborliness in *Memory of a Large Christmas*   133

reflects a clear southern ethos that being well-fed and satisfied bodily supersedes psychological well-being. Benjamin notes that "surrender to the Third, which 'is love itself' can be maintained even when the other fails. . . . The essence of the third position is that we use it to step out of complementary power relations in which we might feel done to by keeping faith with the intention of our connection" (21). Thus, while the sister's interactions with her father (and even with Big Grandma) in this moment do not reflect intersubjective relational practices of being heard and recognized, Smith accords this kind of recognition to her grandmother retrospectively through this memory, thereby creating what Benjamin calls "symbolic thirdness." For Benjamin, the goal of a "*moral Third*—the principle whereby we create relationships in accord with ethical values—[involves] *symbolic thirdness* which includes narration, self-reflection and observation of self and other" (28). When Smith sympathetically narrates Big Grandma's actions in this scene, she opens the space of the symbolic third.

Additionally, Benjamin's analysis suggests that the symbolic thirdness includes (to some extent) the *differentiating Third*, which is "exemplified by the mother's ability to maintain awareness that the distressed child's pain . . . will pass, alongside her empathy with that pain; that is, she is able to hold the tension between her perspective and her child's, her identification with him [or her] and the adult's observational function" (28). Though Benjamin attributes this role to the mother, Little Grandma functions as the differentiating third for Smith in this memoir and in *The Journey*.

Early in *The Journey*, Smith tells the story of Little Grandma killing a panther before it got to her sleeping child by shooting over the baby's head. When asked by the children how she did it, Little Grandma "would laugh and say, You take aim straight at the head, and you pull the trigger, easy" (63). In describing this story and its many retellings, Smith notes that when Little Grandma told it, it served as "a legend of reassurance, a story of human strength able to deal with what comes to a person day by day. . . . The panther is always killed before it reaches the baby. She made sure of it" (63). Smith also references this story in *Memory of a Large Christmas*. Though it seems fleeting, mentioned only briefly as one of the stories Little Grandma tells when she picks out the pecans after the children harvest them, the nature of the story's telling, as well as its placement in the text, suggests that Little Grandma functions as a differential third. When Smith talks about Little Grandma telling the story of the panther in *Memory of a Large Christmas*, it creates an atmosphere of comfort and community with all the children gathered around Little Grandma and sharing in the harvest. Smith also recalls this memory directly before she recounts the details of hog killing, which she describes as an "orgy and holocaust, wild pleasure and terror" (23). The trauma inherent in this description sets the stage for the extended portrayal to follow, so it is unsurprising that Smith grounds the traumatic memory with a memory of the person whom she describes in *The Journey* as follows:

> At these moments when we shrank in sudden fear from life, even from ourselves, Little Grandma called us into her room, drew us close around her hearth, and somehow healed our bruises—not by tearing us away from our mother; no, this was different from two influences pulling a child in opposing directions. For these two women were too harmonious as mother and daughter-in-law ever to be in conflict— though with feelings so different. It was rather that Grandma was a kind of first-aid station, or a Red Cross nurse, who took up where the battle ended, accepting us and our little sobbing sins, gathering the whole of us into her lap, restoring us to health and confidence by her amazing faith in life and in a mortal's strength to meet it. (67)

As the person who can recognize and understand their fears while also reassuring them of their strength to face them, Little Grandma acts as Benjamin's differentiating Third in this text by a clear reference to her in an earlier autobiographical writing.

Little Grandma's stories offer comfort and even confidence to face the trauma of the hog killing, which Smith describes as "death town noticed Ada getting thin, they realized she needed money for food, which prompted them to ask her to sew doll clothing (32–33). With this gesture, Smith's family and others extend to Miss Ada the notion of "the neighbor" as Edkins describes it. Edkins notes that "the person as neighbor develops a stance or comportment . . . that is specific to each person as singularity" and recognizes the Lacanian lack in each person's psychological development, so that one interacts in such a way as to addend to the "self" of the individual rather than the personality "that constitutes neighbor-love" (136). When the people in Smith's town recognize Miss Ada as a "self" and extend "neighbor-love" to her by helping her earn money for food, they preserve her dignity while also solving her problem. Moreover, by not succumbing to shame or guilt in the face of the problem, the townspeople open a space of the Third for their interaction with Miss Ada. They recognize her pain, and they recognize their complicity in it without allowing the shame of that complicity to prevent action. Benjamin notes that when people create a space for communication that steps out of the need for blame and self-justification, they can also enter a space where "being wrong is not so horribly shameful that we cannot own it" (42). When Smith connects her personal story about Jaspers changing the world to the community's story of extending neighborliness to Miss Ada, she demonstrates how the seemingly small relationships of childhood affect a single conscience and all humanity at once.

As with her memory of Jaspers, Smith deftly demonstrates the intimate connections between black and white lives throughout her memoir. In one especially humorous episode, in which her two older brothers conspire with the family cook's grandson, Town, to buy their father a gift worthy of being called an "heirloom," Smith illustrates the intersubjectivity of this family relationship throughout her account. Spying in her persona as "Little Miss Curiosity," Smith notes that as the boys make their plans for obtaining a gift worthy of being called an heirloom, Town suggests that they visit the court of France, saying, "I'm the ambassador from Africa and I have business with

Neighborliness in *Memory of a Large Christmas*

and blood and squeals and glistening steel blades and smoke [that] had driven tranquility off the face of the earth" (25). In the aftermath of such trauma, however, Jaspers offers her the mutual recognition necessary to set the world right again. Smith notes that Old Jaspers calls her "Little Sister" and shows her how to cut a pork chop when

> the big black hand covered the small white hand, and holding firmly to the long steel knife, the two together pressed down down on something, then Jaspers whispered, Hold tight! and you did, and he lifted your hand and his and the knife and came down hard—and lo, the two of you had cut a pork chop. And he was saying softly, I sho do like pork chops, don't you, Little Sister? and you whispered back, I sho do, Jaspers. And the two words had changed the whole world. (26)

In this moment, Jaspers helps to move beyond the differentiating Third, which helps a child feel safe in the face of danger and adds empathy, thereby extending the "one-way recognition of the child's subjectivity . . . [which] is incompatible with an intersubjective theory of development" (38). When Jaspers holds Smith's hand in his and they share a mutual recognition of each other, they create a "shared Third," which validates each person's subjectivity, as well as the mutual intersubjectivity each offers the other. And, as Smith notes, that mutuality not only changes a child's view of himself or herself but can also change the world.

Closely following this account, Smith gives an account of one of the women in town, Miss Ada, who sews dresses for all the little girls' dolls at Christmas. According to Smith, Miss Ada's fiancé died the day before their wedding, and the trauma of his loss left her psychologically fragile, wandering among tombstones in a white dress, talking to herself and laughing or crying at nothing discernible (32). As a single woman without family or a husband to provide for her, Miss Ada soon falls outside the social and political sphere of recognition; she goes "missing" in ways that Jenny Edkins explores in her essay "Time, Personhood, Politics." Smith notes that when people in

Neighborliness in *Memory of a Large Christmas*   137

Louis the Fourteenth—and you two can be my retinue" (38). When Smith's brothers greet the plan with silence, which clearly indicates their dissent, Smith notes that Town recognizes their position and immediately makes accommodation:

> Town, who was the soul of tact, studied the faces of his two friends. With a change of pace, he said, "I know what! I'll be the ambassador from Africa and you be the sheriff and deputy from Dixieland. How'd that be?" "Fine," said his friends. Age Thirteen added slowly, "And we can wear a big silver star—" Town interrupted. "The ambassador can wear one, too. All of us can wear a star," he added tactfully. "You wear a crown," said Age Thirteen. "We wear a silver star." "Nope," said Town firmly. "My name is Town Marshal and that gives me a right to wear a star. All of us can wear one." "That makes sense," said Age Fifteen, who knew when he'd met his match. (38–39)

In Benjamin's notion of complementary relations, otherwise known as "the relation of twoness," she asserts that "there appear to be only two choices: either submission or resistance to the other's demands" (25). However, in a relationship characterized by the reciprocity of what Benjamin calls "the Third," we find a space "of shared communication about reality that tolerates or embraces difference, one which is interpersonally realized as both partners feel freer to think about and comment on themselves and each other" (26). The interaction between the boys, in which they all find mutual dignity in their fantasy of power and representation in the political arena of international relationships, demonstrates Benjamin's Third, here interpersonally realized through mutual comment and reciprocity. Again Smith takes a seemingly benign and humorous moment from childhood and demonstrates the larger implications for interpersonal human relationships. Listening to and engaging with others through reciprocal interactions that accommodate through shared comment on the self and the other lead to more harmonious and empowered interactions for all concerned.

Smith continues to demonstrate how this relationship between her brothers and Town works almost instinctively when she describes how her brothers pass on everything they read to Town, so that he reads exactly the same things that they do, even though the only school available to him meets for a scant three months of the year (48). Moreover, in the easiness of their relationship, Smith recognizes as an adult that "his two friends taught [Town] what they learned each day and he kept right up with them—although, maybe, they didn't know they were teaching and he didn't know he was learning. They just liked to do everything together so they did it" (48). While not overtly commenting on race relations in the South, Smith acknowledges Town as a member of her family and moves past the blame and shame of the American South to show a productive (though by no means perfect) childhood relationship of reciprocity.

After cataloging so many positive memories of shared family traditions, plentitude, and childhood bonding, Smith notes that all Christmases until World War I contained similar qualities. After the war, however, her father lost most of his business interests in Florida, forcing the family to move to their summer home in the mountains of north Georgia. Although Smith claims in *Memory of a Large Christmas* that "there was nothing dismal about that moving, for my father departed like an explorer setting out for an unknown continent" and "succeeded in convincing everybody but Mother that our new life was going to be more interesting than our old" (57), Smith relates quite a contradictory account of the move in a letter to Maxwell Geismar dated January 1961, the same year that she wrote her memoir. In the letter, she tells Geismar:

> The night I was graduated from high school, I came back from the auditorium, changed from my white accordion-pleated dress, . . . and [came] to Clayton, our new home which for a few years had been our summer home. I left that wonderful sixteen-room house in which I was born. . . . We were going to be poor (and I had never been poor); we were going to have a rather bleak life for a while, and I knew it. All I wanted was never to let Mother and Dad know I cared. (214–15)

Neighborliness in *Memory of a Large Christmas* 139

These apparently contradictory representations of her family's changed economic circumstance and subsequent move contain not just the beauty of the ostensible paradox that Smith celebrates regarding this memoir. They also contain the "multiple, disjunctive meanings" that Benjamin claims "may allow for multiple self-states to be present or alternate in awareness." Benjamin notes that "play [or creative expression] allows selves that would otherwise be at war with one another to co-exist, even to co-create together" (192). While Benjamin's discussion centers on the clinical practice, one can easily see how this situation applies to the literary situation in which the author's creative expression puts in conversation the various aspects of her "selves" to create a conversation that allows for a positive self-awareness. Indeed, Tom Haddox notes that Smith would no doubt agree with Schiller's claim that "Man plays only when he is in the full sense of the word a man, and he is only wholly Man when he is playing," because "the aesthetic alone leads to the unlimited" (qtd. in Haddox 54). Smith's "play" in the creative expression of her two selves representing this defining moment in her life creates a third space of multiplicity from which to examine the event—here claiming the positive, as she does with so many of her memories.

Characteristic of the optimistic nature of the piece, Smith spends little time on the particularities of her family's poverty, noting only that their situation was not unique and that it eventually prompted her and her sister to return home to help her parents. Readers familiar with Smith's writings and her personal correspondence will know that such a benign representation once again suggests a form of the creative play noted earlier.[1] Smith extends this positive representation of self when she notes that owing to their financial circumstances, she and her sister had agreed to skip Christmas, affirming to each other that "you don't always have to have Christmas" (59). Though Smith and her sister affirm this commitment, they do not consider their father.

Early in the narrative, Smith notes that each Christmas her father would read the story of Christ's birth from Luke, chapter 2. She contends that for "him it was not only the story of the Christ Child but of Every Child, every new beginning, every new chance for peace on earth" (51). Understanding Christmas as an opportunity to extend peace on earth, Smith's father visits the prisoners working on the state roads who were "staying in two shabby red railroad cars on a siding" (60). He finds the living conditions there so terrible that they are "not fit for animals," never mind humans (60). Recognizing the unnecessary nature of the prisoners' misery, Smith's father seeks to do his own part to salve human suffering by inviting the prisoners to Christmas dinner. This story is arguably one of the most important memories in the book, and I will examine it at length.

When Smith recalls the members of the forty-eight-man chain gang, she notes that "eight of the men were lifers; six of them, in pairs, had their inside legs locked together; ten were killers (one had bashed in his grandma's head), two had robbed banks, three had stolen cars, one had burned down his neighbor's house and barn after an argument, one had raped a girl" (61). Interestingly, she does not reveal where she learns this information. The prison guards who accompany the men to dinner perhaps relayed it to the family, or the men themselves told their stories. Smith does say, however, that during dinner her father spoke with the men, "asking them about their families, telling them a little about his" (62). In the very important work of intersubjective communication, her father *recognizes* his guests. As Benjamin contends, "Recognition becomes an end in itself: human beings want to *share* attention and intentions . . . not only for the sake of state regulation and soothing but also . . . for the sake of *sharing* itself. . . . Recognition involves knowing and being known, . . . when, as Sanders puts it, 'one individual comes to savour the wholeness of another'" (77; italics in original). Without moral judgment or a requirement for justification from the men who came to dinner, Smith's father simply offers and receives human recognition from his *guests*—the term that Smith carefully chooses to describe the men who dined with her family that Christmas.

In Jenny Edkins's work on people who are "missing" within state-sanctioned spaces of power, the men in this chain gang constitute

Neighborliness in *Memory of a Large Christmas* 141

"missing people"—those whose lives operate outside the system of viable personhood and whose selfhood no longer matters to the state, as demonstrated by their living conditions when Smith's father goes to visit them. However, not only does Smith's family welcome these men into their home without moral judgment about their crimes, but they cook their best food and interact with the men as their guests. According to Edkins, "It is precisely the lack or gap between the neighbour-person and the social role he or she is supposed to play in the social or symbolic order that constitutes the neighbour as loveable." She goes on to suggest that we can extend this idea of neighbor as lovable when we "look for such community in the realm of the everyday, in the lives of the oppressed, the missing, the formerly disappeared, the survivors of betrayals" (136, 138). Despite our different contexts, Edkins's point proves instructive for how to read this scene in Smith's memoir. Edkins builds on her definition of neighborliness as an "interaction based on an acknowledgment of finitude, and of what is missing—an acknowledgment of the impossibility of completeness . . . around which each person constitutes a fantasy of subjectivity" to develop her idea of a neighbor as lovable (138). To understand the neighbor-person as lovable, Edkins extends her definition of neighborliness when she says, "It is a taking on, or assumption of, the lack or exception at the heart of what we call social reality, a traversing of the fantasy, and a recognition in self and neighbor" (138). This "taking on" or "recognition" described by Edkins as the foundation of neighborliness or neighbor-love requires the reciprocity that Benjamin elucidates in her notion of the moral Third, which she argues gets expressed through "co-creation—sharing states . . . recognition of other minds through . . . understanding and negotiating differences. All express the position of differentiating without polarizing, connecting without erasing difference" (78). When Smith's family invite a multiracial group of convicts into their home and engage them as guests, they demonstrate Edkins's notion of neighborliness as a way of expressing Benjamin's moral Third. Smith's father addresses the men in familial tones, calling one man "son" (62), and affords them the dignity of helping Smith's mother bring the heavy dishes to serve dinner, not because of compulsion by the guard who accompanies them but because of the desire to help in a familial setting (62). Thus the family extend not only hospitality, which act would constitute mere charity and establish a hierarchical relational dynamic; they also extend the reciprocity of selfhood to the men who dine with them by hearing their stories and telling them their own, by serving them and being served by them.

Indeed, when the chain gang leave and the family reflect on the day later that evening after receiving a letter from Smith's sister, Smith notes that her father expresses pride for how the family has endured their poverty. Moreover, he tells his daughters and his wife: "Those men, today—they've made mistakes. Sure. But I have too. Bigger ones maybe than theirs. And you will. You are not likely to commit a crime but you may become blind and refuse to see what you should look at, and that can be worse than a crime. Don't forget that. Never look down on a man. Never. If you can't look him straight in the eyes, then what's wrong is with you" (63). The notion of acknowledging the flaws in another as equal to one's own, and even seeing one's self in another's moral failings, is crucial to establishing Benjamin's moral Third. She explains that accepting the bad identified in the other into the good identified in the self eliminates the harmful boundaries of the us/them dichotomy that creates a metaphorical (and in some cases) literal space where "only one can live" (223). Moving beyond these complementary relationships into the space of the moral Third allows for the capacity to accept multiple identifications into the psyche, so that one entertains relationships beyond "doer and done to, kill or be killed" (227). Smith details a similar outlook in her "Letter to Mr. Hartley" in 1959, where she contends that learning (about others as well as the self) builds bridges among and between people. She writes, "I think all of life is learning. If you want to close up, you can . . . but if you want to open up, you will be bound to learn to become aware, to reach out for others and toward others. . . . And then there is always what you learn when you build bridges to other people: to one, then

Neighborliness in *Memory of a Large Christmas* 143

to one more, and on and on" (15). The process of bridge building here asserts the kind of interconnectedness Benjamin advocates.

After Smith's father tells her and her sister the importance of accepting people as they are—of seeing themselves in others and looking them in the eye—he goes on to tell them that when the world faces times of change such as those associated with war and economic hardship, people's proclivity for making mistakes increases. He then cautions his daughters not to cling to the mistakes of the past, encouraging them instead to seek change. He tells them that "changing things is mighty risky, but not changing things is worse—that is, if you can think of something better to change to" (63–64). Despite her father's injunction that Smith not "get radical" in her desire for change, this call for a vision about the future echoes her father's perspective about Christmas throughout the narrative. Earlier in the text, when Smith describes her father reading from the biblical account of Christ's birth in Luke 2, she explains that he followed his reading with a prayer in which he "asked [God's] blessing on all who were suffering and in need in every country in the whole world, and then he asked for courage, courage to have vision, for 'without vision the people perish'" (51). As the examples highlighted here show, this philosophy of courage and vision manifests itself through an embodied recognition of people around them in neighborly practices like those shown to Miss Ada and the men in the chain gang.

The book ends with Smith and her sister reflecting on all the Christmases before and recounting the stories retold by Smith in the preceding memoir. After they reminisce and laugh for a while, Smith ends with this final exchange between them:

My sister said softly, "It was a large Christmas."
  "Which one?"
  "All of them," she whispered. (64)

Though the family has just hosted fifty people for dinner and thus had a very large Christmas indeed, what the sisters recall through their memories, and what Smith herself recalls throughout the book, is not just the number of people around any given Christmas table. Rather, they recall the bounty of relationships, of love, and of acceptance—for each other and for those around them.

According to Margaret Rose Gladney, "On a 1962 Christmas card Smith thanked Frank Daniel of the *Atlanta Journal* for his 'elegant piece about my little book' and included the following: 'I shall always be glad I skimmed off so much good, clotted cream from my childhood memories. . . . My own family are deeply moved by the sweet good memories which for so long were hidden behind the tragic ones [of her mother's and father's deaths] about which we all were completely silent'" (Gladney 240). After the main narrative of *Memories of a Large Christmas*, Smith includes a section titled "Christmas Kitchen Fifty Years Ago," in which she describes how her mother and grandmothers, along with the family cook, prepared the large meals her family ate at the Christmas dinners described in the book. She also includes how her mother taught her to bake, as well as a selection of recipes from her family's Christmas table. One of the memories included in this section is of her mother skimming cream from the milk bowls. Smith explains that her mother would "fold heavy yellow cream back from the pale blue milk beneath, then skillfully swoop the thick roll up with her big spoon into the cream bowl. I'd whisper, 'Oh Mama, let's have some hot gingerbread for supper all covered with cream,' and she'd look at me and say 'Sssh . . .' as though the cream were a sleeping baby. She handled it as gently as if it were one" (70). Smith notes that despite her mother's injunction to silence, the hot gingerbread covered in cream nearly always appeared on their dinner table as a treat for them all. The parallel between this image of Smith with her mother skimming cream for a family treat and the notion that this book of her Christmas memories also constitutes the good, clotted cream of her family memories is striking.

As Smith herself noted, the memoir reveals contradictions about her family, but it also reveals contradictions about her relationship with the South. Fred Hobson asserts that Lillian Smith supporters

Neighborliness in *Memory of a Large Christmas* 145

would not contend that she "was always capable of balance . . . [or] of diplomacy" regarding southern race relations (332). And while Smith does not directly address the question of race in this memoir, she does attend to interracial relationships throughout the text; relationships that, while they do not attain the full equality and reciprocity required for Benjamin's moral Third, gesture toward the possibility of neighbor-love and accepting difference in the other as part of an understanding of self. Moreover, Smith extends the same care to her family members with her memories and the stories she tells of them. She does not fool herself or the reader into believing that her family is perfect. In fact, she observers that between her parents "there were thunder and lightning times . . . and silences that raced your heart, but these you didn't think about at Christmas" (34). This book, then, serves not to put a metaphorical bow on the present of happy memories while pretending all is well. Instead I contend that Smith offers these memories to demonstrate the potential in the good memories—in the examples of neighborliness and love that existed in her family and her community.

Tom Haddox and others have noted Pierre Teilhard de Chardin's influence on Smith's thinking and writing. According to Haddox, Smith's writing by the end of *The Journey* reflects this influence in her "implicit call for an authentically normal human development, which works simultaneously toward greater unity and greater personalization—a process both aesthetic and political" (54). For Smith, the process of writing the self included the process of writing humanity. To offer the cream of her family memories alongside the "pale blue" milk of the problems she regularly called out places this memoir as an offering of good faith of the good in the other that she so regularly criticized.

Smith herself contends in *The Journey*:

The importance of breaking the silence lies in our willingness to give up pretensions to a power and perfection we had no right to in the first place. In surrendering pretension—which means abandoning old and beloved defenses—there is real pain. It is not easy. But those who have done so are finding and donating to the world a fresh strength and a new subtle quality of communication which comes because they are in touch with others on the deepest levels of experience. (249)

Smith understood the power of listening in the context of the civil rights movement, as she explains here, and her memoir of Christmas memories demonstrates the power of listening to the past. She understands the power of reclaiming the good—not to rebuild the defenses so long held but to ensure "each partner's survival . . . [by] being changed by the other without collapsing or having one's subjectivity erased" (Benjamin 85). When Smith reclaims her family's (and by extension the South's) humanity and dignity in these memories, she creates the space for both realities to exist and both to be heard.[2]

I do not wish to suggest that Smith's small memoir ceases her call for reform regarding entrenched racial and sexual ideas. Rather, I advocate that the consistent call for courage and vision regarding people and how one relates to them marks Smith's memories in this text, which in turn recuperates those who might formerly have felt attacked and ostracized in her writing. Such acknowledgment and witness bearing hold the potential to move people past the binary thinking "of deserving and discarded in which Only one can live [to one which] requires the vision of a lawful world in which our mutual attachment to all parts of the whole is honored. Both harmers and harmed need the moral Third of 'All can live' to replace the frightening world in which 'Only one can live'" (Benjamin 248). Smith demonstrates that when we recognize the redemptive potential in others while also making space for the alterity that comes from encompassing their sinfulness, we create a moral Third that sees beyond any easy binary.

Neighborliness in *Memory of a Large Christmas*   147

Notes

1. Margaret Rose Gladney notes, for example, that Smith wrote to P. D. East in September 1961, "I am tired of mothering the whole damn South as I have mothered the Smith family for thirty years!" (240–41).

2. Indeed, somewhat in contrast to Hobson's assertions regarding Smith's views of the South, Robert Poister argues that Smith's attitude toward those in Appalachia reveals a kind of growth after her family moved to Georgia when she was a teenager. Over the years, her opinions changed until, as Poister contends, "Appalachia was not only important to Smith's writing and work, but to her life. It shaped her person and her ideas, despite her dislike of the people and the area. Smith's ability to see beyond the stereotypes, to find a more complete view of mountaineers that showed her a people she learned to love, showed in her the capacity to change which she lamented was absent from so much of the South. It was a quality she commended in the people of Clayton" (282).

Works Cited

Benjamin, Jessica. *Beyond Doer and Done To: Recognition Theory, Intersubjectivity and the Third*. Routledge, 2017.

Edkins, Jenny. "Time, Personhood, Politics." *The Future of Trauma Theory: Contemporary Literary Cultural Criticism*, edited by Gert Buelens, Sam Durrant, and Robert Eaglestone, Routledge, 2014, pp. 127–39.

Gladney, Margaret Rose, ed. *How Am I to Be Heard? Letters of Lillian Smith*. U of North Carolina P, 1993.

Haddox, Thomas F. "Lillian Smith, Cold War Intellectual." *Southern Literary Journal*, vol. 44, no. 2, 2012, pp. 51–68.

Hobson, Fred. *Tell about the South: The Southern Rage to Explain*. Louisiana State UP, 1983.

Poister, Robert C. "At Home on the Mountain: Appalachia in Lillian Smith's Life and Work." *Appalachian Journal*, vol. 37, nos. 3–4, 2010, pp. 265–85.

Smith, Lillian. *The Journey*. World Publishing, 1954.

Smith, Lillian. Letter to Alice Shoemaker, October 30, 1965. Gladney, 328–31.

Smith, Lillian. Letter to Bertha Barnett, April 6, 1962. Gladney, 295–97.

Smith, Lillian. Letter to Marvin Rich, December 1, 1961. Gladney, 289–91.

Smith, Lillian. Letter to Maxwell Geismar. *The Winner Names the Age: A Collection of Writings by Lillian Smith*, edited by Michelle Cliff, Norton, 1978, pp. 214–15.

Smith, Lillian. "Letter to Mr. Hartley." *A Lillian Smith Reader*, edited by Margaret Rose Gladney and Lisa Hodgens, U of Georgia P, 2016, pp. 12–16.

Smith, Lillian. *Memory of a Large Christmas*. W. W. Norton, 1961, 1962.

CHAPTER 7

Hatred and Hope in the American South: Rhetorical Excavations in Lillian Smith's *Our Faces, Our Words*

—David Brauer

Lillian Smith's *Our Faces, Our Words* is a mercurial text. Her final monograph does not fit into easy categories but instead challenges the audience to reckon with its evasive characteristics. And these subtleties prove ironic, for Smith does not lack a clear purpose. She wants to awaken her readers to the gross injustices of racial segregation. The text reflects what Jordan Dominy has identified as "Smith's belief that art can bring about social and political change" (37). But Smith uses a serrated edge to cut. In terms of its genre classification, *Our Faces, Our Words* (*OFOW*) may best be understood as a mixed genre, a combination of literary and nonliterary writing juxtaposed with stark images from the civil rights era of the early 1960s. If, as Elizabeth Wardle contends, a genre is a "response to an exigence" (768), then the fact that *OFOW* resists genre classification underscores the complex, layered purposes of Smith's rhetoric. Smith uses conflated genres to attack white supremacy as the ideological base of segregation and to reveal the need for social disruption to effect real change in the American South.

Smith's relative obscurity as a twentieth-century writer offers clues about the challenges that she faced in speaking out on segregation. Despite numerous publications on race, including *Killers of the Dream* and *Strange Fruit*, Smith did not enjoy a situated ethos (see Ratcliffe; Haddox; Brinkmeyer). She experienced the civil rights movement not as a participant but as an observer. Most of her books were met with mixed reviews, and she was generally overlooked by the media as a white, upper-class proponent of civil rights. Moreover, she was a southerner who did not fit in with her culture of origin. As Scott Romine points out, Smith constructed her writerly persona as a "Southern outsider, one who has impeccable credentials as a Southerner but who has eluded Southern constraints on verbal expression" (96). As a woman of independent economic means, Smith was a social insider, but as an ardent supporter of the civil rights movement and an unmarried woman, she was also an outsider. Yet Smith saw how social and ideological privilege determined assumptions about race and segregation, and she dared to think and speak differently. *OFOW* reveals both her awareness of the rhetorical situation and her willingness to resist the status quo and challenge it. Krista Ratcliffe points out Smith's choice to reinvent her ethos on numerous occasions: "No matter how carefully she had crafted her authorial agency, the dominant discursive, readerly, and cultural agencies worked against her. Yet, Smith's experience is not the occasion for despair or the rationale for a retreat into gradualism. It is a model for how a resisting agency may challenge other agencies haunted by whiteness" (111). Smith did not focus primarily on the political elements of the civil rights movement but rather used *OFOW* to highlight the influence of habit, language, and perception in obscuring the impact of segregation on all who participated in it. Instead of being constrained by a situated ethos, Smith applies the need to reinvent her ethos as an opportunity to blur genre distinctions and mix subtle and assertive rhetorical strategies in the text.[1] Ironically, Smith's "lack" of artistic credibility allows her to ignore familiar tactics and to erase her authorial persona from the majority of *OFOW* by speaking through the voices of others.

In fact, the varied backgrounds of the narrators in the monologues provide Smith with one clear avenue toward building her credibility. In speaking through the voices of many, she speaks for all. Smith wants *OFOW* to reflect not simply her perspective, just one of many. The multivoiced aspect of *OFOW* enables Smith to use narrators with different backgrounds and experiences to produce a unified perspective on segregation. In a move of rhetorical prestidigitation, Smith is building her credibility by deliberately obfuscating herself for the majority of the book. Her voice takes center stage in the conclusion, only after the other voices have spoken. Smith knows that if the text reads like the opinion of one southern progressive, then it will likely fail rhetorically. Her credibility rests on presenting her viewpoint as the consensus of the people who understand the civil rights movement best: the participants and the thoughtful observers. If the Aristotelian definition of *ethos* centers on the personality and trustworthiness of the narrator, then Smith seems to invert this strategy; the less her persona dominates the text, the better. Thus Smith shared with her critics the perspective that her role as artist was secondary to her role as a spokesperson for the civil rights movement.

Context has anything but a neutral role in Smith's rhetorical situation. If the rest of mainstream society in the mid-twentieth century looked at both the present and the future as mutual focal points, the South understood itself primarily in relationship to the past. In a 1950 review of *Killers of the Dream*, Margaret Hartley highlights Smith's layered exegesis of southern history: "[The past] contains the suppressed and poisoned emotions of a race, fundamentally generous and kind, which has betrayed itself in oppressing another race and has felt continuously, in every aspect of its life, the results of that betrayal" (146). If slavery was the original sin of the American South, then the fallout of that choice has tainted every element of that society: economic, social, political, educational, relational, psychological. For Smith, this context is something that she needs to make her argument, but it also circumscribes her prospects for effective persuasion. Segregation and racial oppression are not mere elements of southern life. Rather, they are the water in which the fish swim. In a passage from *Killers of the Dream*, Smith explains the fundamental predicament that the past holds for both herself and her southern audience: "We have known guilt without understanding it, and there is no tie that binds men closer to the past and each other than that" (26). The paradox of Smith's rhetorical situation is that her context may neutralize the power of her argument even as she recognizes and attempts to overcome this central impediment. Smith has the unenviable role of the surgeon who must cut out the heart to save the patient.

Smith organizes *OFOW* as a collection of monologues by various figures in the civil rights movement and concludes with a reflective essay on both the previous content and the uncertain future of the movement itself. The monologues develop not as transcriptions but as imagined narrative portrayals of individual experiences. The narrators are both black and white, educated and uneducated, desperate and hopeful. Smith alternates among reflective, philosophical, and narrative-driven sections, but her tone generally remains pointed and aggressive. One of the early monologues, "A Cup of Coffee," records the experience of a black college student who followed the "Greensboro Four" by staging a sit-in that led to the desegregation of local businesses. The following monologue, titled "The Search for Excellence Takes Us to Strange Places," chronicles the thoughts and experiences of a young white woman who has participated in the civil rights movement and endured questioning by police officers about her involvement with the black community. The daughter of a white civic leader who is reluctant to criticize segregation publicly, she symbolizes that hope for change may rely on generations losing their hold on the past. The monologue "Memories: How Sweet and Terrible!" captures the reflections of a self-described "Northern negro," an educated black from the Northeast who moved to Mississippi to help with the movement, bringing an outsider's perspective on the ways in which memory and history undermine the South's ability to change. The narrators of the various monologues do not identify themselves by name. A given narrator's namelessness invites the reader to identify more closely with the narrator in question. Otherwise, knowing the narrator's identity might encourage a critical distance that Smith

Rhetorical Excavations in *Our Faces, Our Words*

sees as counterproductive to her rhetorical purposes. Randall Patton describes Smith as a social activist unique among her historical peers because she "advocated an intensely psychological view of the race problem" (374). The emotional proximity and confrontational nature of *OFOW* fuel its rhetorical impact. Smith does not want any reader to walk away from the text undisturbed or unchanged.

The book's first words, "We slept so long" (13), introduce a dominant motif in *OFOW*. Throughout the text, Smith characterizes the civil rights movement as a kind of awakening. Both philosophical and spiritual, this awakening began in the black community and spread eventually to the white community. This awakening involved a recognition that racial segregation had dehumanized black Americans. If they were legally "human," they were a lesser kind of human than the whites with whom they interacted in public spaces. But Smith also argues that segregation harms whites because it weakens their capacity for empathy and community with minorities. Judy Holiday explains that Smith was influenced by Gandhi "to understand that all subject positions are victimized within a hierarchical system" (40–41). Though Smith laid the blame at the feet of the dominant race, her vision for change draws on and reinforces the centrality of the common good.

Smith resists the detached points of view common in traditional journalistic or academic strategies of persuasion. Instead she presents lived experience as her rhetorical "proof." Because she avoids a philosophical approach, Smith eliminates the psychic distance that might enable the reader to avoid moral culpability. The text is not for someone else; it is for you—*de te fabula narratur*. The text itself eludes summary and conceptualization. Yes, we may parse the text and its content, but Smith does not want us to explain it and thus explain it away. Smith's own purpose is to show rather than to explain. As Holiday explains, Smith does not view segregation as a set of laws that operate at a safe distance from the reader. Instead segregation exemplifies what Holiday terms a "hierarchical thinking" that operates as "a perceptual system that inhibits the accommodation of difference while enabling people to feel justified in their abjection of and violence toward others" (70). Smith furnishes her argument with testimonies and evidence in the form of examples, examples of real lives in the civil rights movement. The narrators of these monologues reveal how segregation has shaped their thinking and victimized them, and their collective anger, frustration, and guilt indicate the psychological and political damage done by this hierarchical system. From Smith's perspective, the insidious nature of segregation highlights the shortcomings of a persuasive strategy centered on logos. Because Smith views racism in part as a thinking problem, she deploys pathos as a central rhetorical strategy. Because white supremacy manifests as a kind of twisted logos that resists other logical arguments, she cannot rely on logos to carry the audience to the conclusion that she desires. Even so, logos has a critical role here; just as white supremacy has caused racism and segregation, her argument must address the conceptual underpinnings of the civil rights movement and drive the audience to ideological and social transformation.

Smith's rhetorical strategies disclose an unconventional application of Aristotelian rhetorical guidelines and thus create a text that resists ideological labels or easy summaries. If King's "Letter from Birmingham Jail" was an argument for the learned and the attentive, *OFOW* proves a far more unsettling experience.[2] Smith recognizes that "nice talk" about segregation has served to appease and entrench southern bigotry rather than to effect change. The diction reveals her anxieties about the future of the movement and the outcome of the battle for civil rights. As a result, the text stops just shy of expressing outright hostility toward white southerners. While she condemns the violence and militancy of Malcolm X, Smith champions the disruptive practices of CORE and other groups working picket lines and conducting sit-ins. Robert Brinkmeyer observes that Smith had already broken with many liberals of her day, as she viewed their "gradualism . . . as a profound failure in leadership that was a disastrous impediment to change" (176). Smith understood the value of cultural disruption because she recognized the underpinnings of segregation. Segregation

Rhetorical Excavations in *Our Faces, Our Words* 155

was ineluctably connected to white supremacy, which itself rested on economic and cultural privilege that the dominant race did not want to lose. But if white supremacy was championed by the Ku Klux Klan, it was accepted by both blacks and moderate whites. White supremacy had become an ontological prison. Holiday points out that "privilege does not necessarily operate on the conscious level, and most often operates at the level of the habitual and embodied" (47). Smith could not illuminate the problem through direct assertion. Rather, she needed her readers to begin to question their own assumptions about the nature of segregation and its roots in the invisible, unquestioned elements of lived experience. Smith wants to change the mind of her reader, but she also wants to disturb them so that they may see their moral culpability in the system of white supremacy, break down that system, and replace it with a system of empathy and equality.

The figures who populate the monologues and the pictures in *OFOW* do not represent the celebrities of the movement. Likewise, Smith largely avoids dramatizing the era's more famous events. She resists what Charles Payne refers to as a "top-down" narrative of the civil rights movement (Lawson and Payne 110–11). To be fair, she does lionize Martin Luther King Jr. and Rosa Parks as key public figures in the struggle (107–8). But Smith recognizes even during the movement that it has layers and that much of its work may be obscured by the media even as it is revealed in newspaper stories and, with increasing significance, on nightly television. For all the known players, there are thousands who remain unknown. Smith favors the latter without ignoring the role of the former. Women and men, young and old, high school graduates and college professors, all have a part to play. In short, Smith presents the movement as truly democratic, a labor of ordinary people working together for one goal, even if the means and impressions proved disparate.

The monologues in *OFOW* have a claustrophobic intimacy that draws the reader into the pained experience of black Americans and those who fight on their behalf. Smith and her narrators recognize that segregation is both a political and a relational problem to be solved. For the most part, Smith emphasizes the relational over and against the political. The text levels plenty of criticism toward George Wallace and senators from southern states who favored gradual changes to the system, but Smith argues, directly at times, that segregation will not end until people relate to one another differently. In the conclusion, she argues that "it is not enough to give [blacks] hand-outs of food, things, books; one must give them concern, understanding—this is the only bridge these tremulous, quietly raging people can walk across" (115). If segregation is a sociological and political phenomenon to be comprehended and resolved through such avenues, then racism is essentially cultural, personal, and phenomenological. The segregated South was a kind of social Being, a shared experience by both blacks and whites that few recognized as unjust. They had lived it so long that they did not see it. Smith's rhetorical strategies indicate her awareness that change would not come easily and needed catalysts to overturn the apple cart of tradition. Smith describes the symbolic role of Rosa Parks in these words: "For Mrs. Rosa Parks, the moment came . . . as she sat in the bus, tired from a day's work: she was asked to move back, and suddenly her entire life came together, fused in one terrific moment of decision, and she said 'No.' That word, 'No,' which she had not planned to say, did not know she was about to say, changed the tempo of racial change for our entire nation" (108). For Smith, *OFOW* embodies the rhetoric of "No," a persuasive refusal to accept segregation as acceptable. Parks's response articulates a negative epiphany, a glaring recognition that everything one knows is wrong and that, by consequence, everything must change.

On the surface of the text, Smith appears to follow the standard narrative of the civil rights movement: it was a decade old, it was driven by celebrities like MLK who were palatable to whites, and it was simply about better communication and understanding between blacks and whites. Underneath the surface, though, Smith attacks the assumptions of her white neighbors. For Smith, the movement began not in 1955 but "since the Civil War" and the wounds caused by Reconstruction, as "protest [has never] ceased entirely" (109).[3] In a moment of ideological prescience, she also acknowledges the social construction of race in citing "studies on all aspects of this thing we call 'race'" (109). Though Smith occasionally isolates incorrect "facts" and wrong ideas, she views white supremacy as an epistemological and ontological system that shapes baseline assumptions and ways of living. Her oeuvre worked against that system. In a review of *How Am I to Be Heard?*, Smith's collected letters, Robert Brinkmeyer explains her artistic philosophy: "Creative endeavor, with its motion outward, worked against segregation (understood, in the psychological sense Smith used it, as the withdrawal from life), with its motion inward" (175). To put it simply, Smith offers a countercultural vision for the American South. Near the end of the book, she develops an analogy designed to shock "genteel" southern audiences: "And perhaps we should remember that it takes time to recover from drug addiction; and many whites are addicted to White Supremacy; it has affected minds, emotions, values. The whole country is suffering from withdrawal pains" (123).[4] Despite the persistent feeling that nothing can change in the South, the violence and obscene injustice of segregation thwart the South's ability to function as an effective society. But Smith challenges the notion that culpability might be limited to the South. This addiction has affected every region, every person, at every level of experience. In applying the analogy of addiction, she illuminates the simultaneously damnable and tragic circumstances in which the nation finds itself. Race relations provide the evidence of a corruption that has worked through the entire culture. And Smith seems convinced that the necessary change comes with a violence that may prove more disruptive than the unrest of the movement itself. For her, the unrest and tension are part of the process of cultural redemption, not its fallout, but the movement must endure the threat of irremediable chaos.[5]

In spite of the wide-eyed emotions at play, Smith does include some rhetoric of the parlor; she references Teilhard de Chardin, Buber, Tillich, and others. Teilhard de Chardin proved a significant influence

158   David Brauer

on Smith's thinking: in separate personal letters, she describes *The Phenomenon of Man* as "a terrific book—maybe the greatest of our times" and "the book that has perhaps influenced me most in recent years" (*How* 285, 311). While she does not wish to philosophize her subject or turn segregation into an abstraction, she recognizes the influence of idealist philosophy and twentieth-century theology on the movement. For Smith, these writers provided a way into a different mind-set and inspired participants in the movement. These passages of philosophical reflection demonstrate the intellectual seriousness with which Smith treated her subject. In "A Cup of Coffee," the narrator notes that he had been reading J. D. Salinger's *Franny and Zooey* in his college dorm when one of his friends suggested that "maybe we'd better read Camus' *The Fall*" because the latter resonated with their experience more accurately (29). For this narrator, words matter, whether spoken or written. The narrator begins with a memory of words his uncle spoke to him when he was only six years old, words about the "facts of life": "The most important fact for you, Jim, is that you are a Negro. . . . You're as good as anybody technically, but you are not, actually, until you get your rights as an American. White folks are not going to give them to you even though they belong to you. Remember: they stole 'em from you. Remember: folks don't like to return what they steal. You'll have to take 'em back" (24). Now a college student, the narrator hears one friend telling another friend that his mom had fainted after a long night at work because she could not buy a cup of coffee—she was not allowed in the coffee shop because she was black. The narrator records his reaction: "I closed the book. To hell with *Franny and Zooey*" (27). As he describes his personal transformation in joining the sit-ins, he explains how his mind was changing: "I knew about Negro slums, Harlem, South Side but thought about it in the same way most white boys think about slums and bad housing for whites. I was *sound asleep*, let me settle for that. . . . Well—we were waking up" (28–29). The narrator was ready to trade in his college books to make sure that no black woman ever endured such social privation again. Once he understood that the battle was

Rhetorical Excavations in *Our Faces, Our Words* 159

about human dignity, nothing else mattered. This monologue allows Smith to demonstrate a central assumption of her argument: the black community needed to recognize the injustices of segregation no less than their white counterparts.

Through the narrative monologue, Smith highlights the impact of the written word on readers; the best books both reflect what we know and push us to something else. Thus the narrator of "Memories: How Sweet and Terrible!" cites Teilhard de Chardin's blend of idealistic philosophy and religion in *The Phenomenon of Man* as a framework for understanding the possibilities for societal evolution in twentieth-century America (65–66). The narrator, a PhD-educated northern black, offers a philosopher's perspective on the movement. From the beginning of his monologue, he resists connecting the movement with an ideology: "Labels seem irrelevant to me because what we are involved in is life itself: we are asking for more life as human beings; we are asking for freedom to breathe as men, to grow as children" (65). A reader of books and observer of life, the narrator's detached engagement with southern culture in Mississippi, where he has come to aid the movement, enables him to diagnose the underpinnings of segregation. As he explains, the situation is as obvious, and as complicated, as history itself: "Those southerners are tied and tangled in a web of common memories they can't escape and don't want to escape" (67). These memories often trigger "surges of hate and guilt" (70), emotions that cloud judgment and complicate the relationships between blacks and whites, even those working together to end segregation. For this narrator, and for Smith, the goal is human relationships, and rights are but the means to that end. The narrator describes his work: helping blacks to develop literacy skills and job skills that will give them a meaningful future. If the public face of the movement belongs to those who march and speak, it also needs those who ponder: "So, maybe, the Movement can take a few 'monks,' a few poets and scholars of both races who are aware of where demagoguery with its half-truths and exaggerations leads the masses and knowing this, who try to inject a bit of wisdom and perspective into these wild, tumultuous affairs" (74).[6] This narrator captures Smith's dual purposes in *OFOW*, to shock and to invoke reflection. In this monologue, Smith argues, albeit indirectly, that civil rights and literacy share a familial relationship: the right words may change our perception, which in turn may change our thinking, which in turn may change the way we live. We read many books, but some books read us. For Smith, the second kind is the seed of transformative education and lasting progress.

One of Smith's main assumptions rests on the problem of understanding segregation. Simply put, southerners either misunderstand segregation or fail to see it at all. Smith spends rhetorical capital attempting to help the reader *see* segregation through new eyes. But the act of perception soon gives way to conceptualization—for Smith, these two activities never remain separate for long. And her definition of segregation trades an ideological framework for a philosophical one. Erik Bachman clarifies Smith's choice in the matter:

> For Smith, "segregation" symptomatically and symbolically refers to a truly sublime set of associations, ranging from the localized and ephemeral matters pertaining to the prospects of desegregation in the mid-century U.S. South all the way up to the cosmic evolutionary destiny of the human being as such. Perhaps even more strikingly, however, she insists here that if the struggle for racial desegregation has any meaning at all, then that meaning must be understood to derive from the small part it plays in the further integration of man's species-being (in overcoming "dehumanization"). (161)

Dehumanization in its various forms (war, racism, bigotry, violence, oppression, slavery, etc.) has played a defining role in human history. If the human species would evolve socially, it must recognize these tendencies and overcome them. Segregation is thus not simply about blacks and whites in the American South but rather about all of us. This is a world-historical moment that we cannot afford to get wrong.

It may well be that in Smith's tense engagement of the moment in which American society finds itself, she reveals anxieties about the timing of her book. In this sense, Smith reflects directly on rhetorical *kairos* and its importance in persuasion. Ten years after her appropriately titled *Now Is the Time*, which reflected on the Supreme Court decision in *Brown v. Board of Education*, OFOW reckons with the protest era of the civil rights movement. Now that the black community has awakened to the injustices of segregation and young whites have joined the movement, Smith recognizes that the debate has entered a more tense and hostile stage. And Smith fears that the movement and its moment of opportunity have been compromised by a group she identifies as "the Intruders," likely a reference to Malcolm X and the Nation of Islam, though Smith never names this group directly, whom she describes as a "few half-mad, foolish people who have lost their inner control and good judgment" (123, 124). While the "Intruders" have created turmoil in the civil rights movement itself, the situation is also poisoned by the "group of whites who cling to their Whiteness," the Ku Klux Klan and other overtly racist white groups who oppress blacks and stoke the fires of racial hatred (124). Because of these two groups, Smith fears that the moment will pass before its promise is fulfilled.

Smith seems faced with a nearly impossible rhetorical situation: the South is defined by an intractable mind-set that limits its self-awareness and capacity for change. In the last paragraph of *OFOW*, she warns the reader: "We, as a people, could be confronted soon by a series of catastrophes. Whether this happens depends on the wisdom of responsible Negroes but more, much more on what every responsible white American does next" (128). As Smith knows, the movement is fraught with possibility, for good or for ill. It may bring reconciliation, harmony, and the end of segregation, or it may bring wounds that never heal. It seems clear that Smith had wrestled to maintain a hopeful attitude; one scholar noted in a 1962 article that "*Strange Fruit* [Smith's 1944 novel on interracial romance] offers little hope for the future" (Marcus 615). But the act of artistic creation and rhetorical purpose would indicate that she has willed herself to hope. Smith calls on the reader to redeem the moment. Her final sentence articulates the possibilities: "One thing is certain in a plexus of uncertainties and that is, our encounter with the future cannot be evaded, it must be met by both the artist and the scientist in us, by our deep intuitions and our rigorously proved knowledge—and by the human being in us, too, that creature who knows the power of compassion, the potency of a strange love that keeps reaching out to bind one man to another" (128). Though the moment of her writing was characterized by violence and alienation, Smith chooses to believe in the power of a "strange love" that may overcome the forces that drive humans apart. For this reason, she believes that her message may reach its target, that *kairos* has not passed her by.

Adding another layer of depth and rhetorical immediacy are the pictures that Smith intersperses with the text itself. J. L. Lemke explains the subtle importance of juxtaposing text with image: "Meanings in multimedia are not fixed and additive (the word meaning plus the picture meaning), but multiplicative (word meaning modified by image context, imaged meaning modified by textual context), making a whole far greater than the sum of its parts" (283). In mixing text with image, *OFOW* pursues a gestalt effect. One early picture shows a huddle of police officers near a group of sit-in protesters in a luncheonette (26), and a later picture captures rows of black men in suits participating in the March on Washington (52). In the former image, the officers occupy the right foreground of the picture, one officer standing with hands on hips, all looking away from the group of formally dressed black protesters who take up the left background. Fluorescent tube lights shine down on the scene, illuminating the tension between the two groups and revealing an open space in the luncheonette separating the protesters and the officers, a space symbolizing their mutual alienation. In the latter image, the marchers wear business suits and striped ties, walking together in rows, their postures stern and upright. One marcher carries an American flag, and another carries a sign that reads "Goldwater '64, Bread and Water

'65, Hot Water '66." Their faces express not anger but communal encouragement and firm resolve. Meanwhile the city buildings in the background call to mind the public space shared by both the protesters and their observers. These pictures are not mere window dressing; rather, the images contextualize the monologues and aid the reader in visualizing the experiences articulated by a given narrator. Because the images are not captioned, their connection to the text proves indirect, their meaning suggested rather than explained. Careful students of the civil rights movement would doubtless identify a few places and events, but many prove less recognizable. Readers are invited to interpret the images as they see fit. In organizing the book this way, Smith asks her readers to practice literacies that see the relationship between words and images even when she does not guide the reader with identifying marks or comments.

Smith highlights the power of the media in shaping public perception about the civil rights movement. In her concluding reflective essay, she writes, "Perhaps more than all else, was the effect television had on us in our homes and on the news gatherers; where once newspapers had played down incidents, smothered stories that should have been told, television met the challenge with startling directness and forced newspapers to tell things as they are" (109–10). Smith's rhetorical exigence is one of frustration and urgency—too few Americans see or recognize the dehumanizing effects of segregation and have communicated indifference to the protests against it. By incorporating images so frequently in her text, she acknowledges that words alone may not suffice in meeting the demands of her rhetorical situation. The images here depict the dramatic and the mundane alike; we see blacks in sit-ins, blacks assaulted by police officers, blacks in rural poverty, whites in rural poverty, police officers with smug expressions, black women wearing words of protest on their clothing. Like the monologues, the images are close, intimate, all too willing to invade our personal space. Some show moments of racial interaction and even reconciliation, but most are discomfiting in their portrayal of the segregated American South in the early 1960s. Even so, the book contains few if any images of direct violence. Irit Rogoff has connected "the emergence of visual culture" in the mid-twentieth century with "the epistemological denaturalization of inherited categories" (16). Smith alternates images of segregation with images of solidarity and community to challenge the audience's assumptions about what the South is and what it should or could become. Instead of filling in the gaps of the text, these images provide rhetorical ellipses, inviting the reader to conclude the thought process that Smith has begun in the written text.

Keith Kenney has connected images to rhetoric by identifying them as representing an epideictic genre "because evocative words and images are used to display values rather than to force audiences to submit to the power of cold logic" (68). Far from the ceremonial rhetoric that Aristotle used to define his term, epideictic rhetoric may not be connected to celebration or reflection. Instead it suggests and reflects themes and associations for the audience rather than offering a straight-line claim about its subject matter. Smith offers no pictures of Martin Luther King Jr., George Wallace, or Rosa Parks, figures whose "meaning" was already known and could thus be dismissed as familiar by the reader. Instead we see anonymous protesters, students, and citizens, in classrooms, on the streets, and on porches. Only the three victims of the Freedom Summer murders (James Chaney, Andrew Goodman, and Michael Schwerner) are recognizable without a caption (98). Smith trades icons of the movement so popularized in newspapers and television news for the unknown and the unnamed. As a rhetorical device, these images apply the power of suggestion to undercut the epistemological boundaries of white supremacist thought.

In *OFOW*, Smith offers a counternarrative of the civil rights movement to the narrative fostered by journalists, politicians, and racist organizations like the Ku Klux Klan. Both blacks and whites have been lulled to sleep by these perceptions and distortions of segregation, and Smith clearly believes that her text can play a role in helping both blacks and whites to awaken from their sleep. The irony of Smith's rhetorical situation lies with a clear sense on her part that "civil talk" was not enough to turn the tide of American history in favor of the movement. As such, traditional rhetoric was limited in its effectiveness; something else must be done. At points in *OFOW*, Smith champions disruptive techniques like sit-ins and marches and all but condones violence as a natural outgrowth of segregation, insensitivity, and injustice. While she would like to appeal to the better angels of the American conscience, she recognizes the difficult choice facing the movement: it could engage in yet more "dialogue," or it could have a chance to succeed. Like the protests, *OFOW* is an action designed to create pressure that would in turn create change. Charles Payne offers context on the multivalent character of protest during the civil rights movement: "Direct action was a two-pronged strategy. It was certainly a moral appeal, but it also meant directly interfering with the life of a community" (Lawson and Payne 117). The negation of psychic distance between writer and subject that characterizes *OFOW* enables Smith to voice her solidarity with both the message and the tactics of the movement.

Readers of the twenty-first century may miss a central element of Smith's argument: the tension in the legal-moral axis. While many modern protesters strive for political and legal solutions to injustice, Smith saw the civil rights movement differently. For her and many in the movement, racial discrimination was primarily a moral issue. As such, the text never appeals to lawmakers to solve the problem, though surely they had their part to play. In *Killers of the Dream*, Smith clarifies her perspective on political solutions to segregation: "I believe individuals not connected with politics can do far more than politicians do. It is more urgent to change men's beliefs than to pass legislation though I think both necessary" (3). The primary actors of this play live not in Washington but in one's neighborhood, on one's street, in one's home. As Thomas Haddox has noted, Smith believed that "because its genesis is individual, totalitarianism can only be combated individually" (56). The narrator of "What Do We Want" frames the movement thus: "Is it a revolution? I don't know.

Certainly not a political one. Maybe it is a spiritual one" (61). Supreme Court rulings had done little to change the facts on the ground for black Americans, and the duplicity of many national politicians had left them cold. In a 1955 review of *Now Is the Time*, Ralph McGill captures Smith's perspective on the public's reaction to court decisions in pointing out that "it is up to the people whether 'the change,' which is to say acceptance of the Court's principle, be brought about slowly or quickly" (492). The narrators of the monologues in *OFOW* had one thing in common: instead of waiting for change, they had all decided to take action, whether large or small. From sit-ins to preaching to marching to organizing, these voices captured the people who had mobilized in the civil rights movement. At the end of "What Do We Want," the narrator clarifies the goal: "Oh, yes—your question. What do we want? *Dignity*" (62). The answer proves simple but almost mystifying in its assumptions. These voices do not want merely changed laws but changed minds and changed perspectives, for Smith insinuates that without the latter, the former would serve little purpose. The narrators in *OFOW* seek a modern Great Awakening of racial equality.[7]

Though pathos has the most visible presence of the Aristotelian appeals, Smith's development of ethos may prove the most critical of the text. Smith's application of this artistic proof draws less from Aristotle and more from Cicero and Quintilian.[8] Smith appropriates Cicero in focusing on the civic role of rhetoric, on its power to improve society, but she also borrows from Quintilian the rhetorical power of the virtuous orator. Smith recognizes the need for civic discourse to address social issues; as her publication history indicates, she spent much of her life making public arguments about racism and segregation. But Smith also understands that "good words" should simultaneously produce goodwill in an audience and reflect the ethically sound intentions of the narrator (Atwill 30). Like Cicero, Smith uses rhetoric to address cultural flash points; like Quintilian, she uses rhetoric to promote virtue. Her tone discloses anger and frustration, but she does not attempt to shame her readers. Instead she hoped to educate them much as a teacher would in addressing students. The organization and genre elements of *OFOW* make it seem sui generis, but Smith draws on Greco-Roman humanism for her understanding of the role of public discourse and the role of the socially conscious writer. If Smith's focal point was southern society and its possible transformation, she also recognized the need to develop her own credibility as the authorial voice behind *OFOW*. Above all, Smith was a twentieth-century humanist, for she believed in the power of ideas and of education (see Holiday; Patton) to shape the individual and, in turn, to shape the culture at large. If she could "borrow" credibility from Teilhard de Chardin, from Rosa Parks, and from the voices in the monologues, she could in turn use her rhetorical capital to promote justice and help American society change for good.

In sections like the final "fictional" monologue, titled "You Think about the Three Who Were Killed," Smith communicates the reflections of a southern pastor as he thinks about the murders of James Chaney, Andrew Goodman, and Michael Schwerner. The incident marked one of the darkest and most disturbing moments of the civil rights era: three young activists, two black and one white, were murdered by white supremacists in Mississippi. For Smith, perhaps the most unsettling aspect of segregation centered on the taking of innocent life. But even worse was the reaction to such heinous crimes: not outrage, but indifference. The preacher who speaks this monologue opines on his own sense of responsibility: "And I get up on Sunday in my pulpit and try to say the truth. I look down on those glazed, smooth faces of the indifferent ones, and my heart sickens. Something tells me to go easy, be tactful, be gentle, and something else in me that I think is closer to Jesus Christ tells me to drive these indifferent ones, these dead souls, out of His temple" (100). The question for Smith in *OFOW* seems to be simple: what will change segregation? She offers an answer but fears that few in an obdurate society will hear her. The tension between exigence and context drives Smith to the edge of despair. In this monologue, the preacher articulates the heat of morally righteous fury that may prove the only means of

168   David Brauer

driving out the wickedness of white supremacy and its multivalent effects on minds, hearts, and souls. *OFOW* is Smith's sermon of fire.

Lillian Smith has no misgivings about her audience or about the continued challenges that will face the civil rights movement, and she delivers a message that proves both direct and slanted in its rhetorical strategies. Unlike many voices of protest in the twenty-first century, she calls not for political solutions but for personal ones. Real change, the change that Smith beckons in *OFOW*, comes not from the halls of a lawmaking body but from homes and communities. The issue may seem "public," but for Smith, segregation and prejudice are always and only personal in their causes and their effects. As Brinkmeyer explains, "Near the end of her life . . . [Smith] looked hopefully toward a new era of humanity's spiritual evolution, an age in which people committed themselves not to ideologies but human relationships" (178–79). Smith hoped that her text might catalyze such an evolution. The narratives that she tells are intertwined with hope and desperation, love and anger. Like Langston Hughes, Smith understands that a dream deferred may finally explode. At the time of her writing in 1964, the outcome of the civil rights movement was still in doubt, and the tense mixture of hope and anxiety reflects the state of flux that characterized that historical moment. Ironically enough, it was the Civil Rights Act of the following year that would help to solidify the gains of the movement that she champions in *OFOW*. The emotional intensity and visceral pain of Smith's tone may explain why this text did not become an icon of the civil rights movement, but its multilayered approach to public rhetoric makes it an important cultural artifact for students of the period. For students of historical rhetoric, Smith's text exemplifies how a narrator may combine direct and indirect tactics to address shared guilt and the need for wholesale cultural transformation.

Notes

1. Smith draws her understanding of rhetoric in part from Aristotle, who defined the *artistic proofs* as the strategies of persuasion that require the speaker to identify strategies that will enable them to develop an effective argument. Specifically, Aristotle distinguished *artistic proofs* from *inartistic proofs*, bare facts and information that a speaker might include to support an argument. The artistic proofs include *ethos*, the speaker's credibility; *logos*, the appeals to logic and reason; and *pathos*, the appeals to experience, values, and emotions. See Aristotle, *On Rhetoric*, book 1, chap. 2.

2. Smith and Martin Luther King Jr. shared a mutual fondness for each other's commitment to the civil rights movement. King identifies Smith by name in "Letter from Birmingham Jail" in his list of "white brothers" who "have grasped the meaning of this social revolution and have committed themselves to it" (274).

3. Elsewhere Smith spoke of the willingness to foment anxieties about race relations and miscegenation as a kind of "trickery" that politicians used to shape public perceptions in the South. Smith described this false representation of race as "the juggling of spurious fears with spurious hopes and spurious accusations and calling the mixture a 'new life for our people'" (258). See "Are We Still Buying a New World with Old Confederate Bills?"

4. In her essay "The Right Way Is Not a Moderate Way," Smith compares white supremacy to cancer, a malady she knew all too well: "The tragic fact is, neither cancer nor segregation will go away while we close our eyes. Both are dangerous diseases that have to be handled quickly and skillfully because they spread, they metastasize throughout the organism" (225).

5. Smith's perspectives on the implications of white supremacy extended to the international stage. In an August 1949 editorial, she asserted that the United States squandered an opportunity to help China reject Maoist totalitarianism because of the United States' own myopic views on race: "We could have sold the idea of democracy to those millions of people but we were too busy making them buy white supremacy" (154).

6. In a commencement speech at Kentucky State College in 1951 titled "Ten Years from Today," Smith pleads with artists to use their rhetorical and aesthetic skills to challenge racism and advocate for civil rights. Though she hopes for change, she also warns her fellow artists that "time is important" and that they must recognize the significance of the times in which they live: "What a sad and tragic thing this will be in our South if those who are gifted with words stay silent" (672).

7. In identifying Smith's vision as a kind of "Great Awakening," I call to mind earlier religious revivals in American history. Smith articulates a cultural transformation fueled in part by shared religious beliefs and values.

8. Building on the teachings of Aristotle, Cicero emphasized the importance of rhetoric for developing civic virtues and enhancing public discourse. As a subtle contrast to Cicero, Quintilian emphasized the credibility of the speaker as central

to effective rhetoric; hence his oft-cited definition of rhetoric as the "good person speaking well." Smith's posture vis-à-vis the civil rights movement reflects the vision of Cicero and Quintilian. See Cicero, *The Orator*, books 1–2; and Quintilian, *The Institutes of Oratory*, books 1–2.

Works Cited

Aristotle, *On Rhetoric*, translated by George A. Kennedy, Oxford UP, 1991.

Atwill, Janet. *Rhetoric Reclaimed: Aristotle and the Liberal Arts Tradition*. Cornell UP, 1998.

Bachman, Erik. *Literary Obscenities: U.S. Case Law and Naturalism after Modernism*. Pennsylvania State UP, 2018.

Brinkmeyer, Robert. "Hearing Lillian Smith." *Virginia Quarterly Review*, vol. 71, no. 1, 1995, pp. 173–79.

Cicero. *Of Oratory and Orators*, translated and edited by J. S. Watson, Southern Illinois UP, 1970.

Dominy, Jordan. "Reviewing the South: Lillian Smith, *South Today*, and the Origins of Literary Canons." *Mississippi Quarterly*, vol. 66, no. 1, 2013, pp. 29–50.

Gladney, Margaret Rose, ed. *How Am I to Be Heard? Letters of Lillian Smith*, U of North Carolina P, 1993.

Gladney, Margaret Rose, and Lisa Hodgens, eds. *A Lillian Smith Reader*. U of Georgia P, 2016.

Haddox, Thomas. "Lillian Smith, Cold War Intellectual." *Southern Literary Journal*, vol. 44, no. 2, 2012, pp. 51–68.

Hartley, Margaret. "Strange Legacy." *Southern Review*, vol. 35, no. 2, 1950, pp. 145–48.

Holiday, Judy. *Reframing the Problem of Difference: Lillian Smith and Hierarchical Politics of Difference*. PhD diss., Arizona State University, 2012.

Kenney, Keith. "Building Visual Communication Theory by Borrowing from Rhetoric." *Journal of Visual Literacy*, vol. 22, no. 1, 2002, pp. 53–80.

King, Martin Luther, Jr. "Letter from Birmingham Jail." *Best American Essays of the Century*, edited by Joyce Carol Oates, Houghton Mifflin, 2000, pp. 263–79.

Lawson, Steven F., and Charles Payne. *Debating the Civil Rights Movement, 1945–1968*. Rowman & Littlefield, 1998.

Lemke, J. L. "Multimedia Literacy: Transforming Meanings and Media." *Handbook of Literacy and Technology: Transformations in a Post-typographic World*, edited by David Reinking, Michael C. McKenna, Linda D. Labbo, and Ronald D. Kieffer, Lawrence Erlbaum Associates, 1998, pp. 293–301.

Marcus, Fred. "*Cry, the Beloved Country* and *Strange Fruit*: Exploring Man's Inhumanity to Man." *English Journal*, vol. 51, no. 9, 1962, pp. 609–16.

McGill, Ralph. "A Matter of Change." *Celebrating the Georgia Writers Hall of Fame*, special issue of *Georgia Review*, vol. 63, no. 3, 2012, pp. 492–94.

Patton, Randall. "Lillian Smith and the Transformation of American Liberalism, 1945–1950." *The Diversity of Southern Gender and Race: Women in Georgia and the South*, special issue of *Georgia Historical Quarterly*, vol. 76, no. 2, 1992, pp. 373–92.

Quintilian. *Institutes of Oratory; or, Education of an Orator*. Translated by John Selby Watson (1856), CreateSpace, 2015.

Ratcliffe, Krista. "Eavesdropping as Rhetorical Tactic: History, Whiteness, and Rhetoric." *Journal of Advanced Composition*, vol. 20, no. 1, 2000, pp. 87–119.

Rogoff, Irit. "Studying Visual Culture." *The Visual Culture Reader*, edited by Nicholas Mirzoeff, Abingdon-on-Thames, Routledge, 1998, pp. 14–26.

Romine, Scott. "Framing Southern Rhetoric: Lillian Smith's Narrative Persona in *Killers of the Dream*." *South Atlantic Review*, vol. 59, no. 2, 1994, pp. 95–111.

Smith, Lillian. "Are We Still Buying a New World with Old Confederate Bills?" Gladney and Hodgens, 256–62.

Smith, Lillian. *Killers of the Dream*. 2nd ed., W. W. Norton, 1994.

Smith, Lillian. *Our Faces, Our Words*. W. W. Norton, 1964.

Smith, Lillian. "The Right Way Is Not the Moderate Way." Gladney and Hodgens, 223–29.

Smith, Lillian. "A Southerner Talking, August 20, 1949." Gladney and Hodgens, 154–55.

Smith, Lillian. "Ten Years from Today." *Vital Speeches of the Day*, August 1951, pp. 669–72.

Wardle, Elizabeth. "'Mutt Genres' and the Goal of FYC: Can We Help Students Write the Genres of the University?" *College Composition and Communication*, vol. 60, no. 4, 2009, pp. 765–89.

Contributors

Tanya Long Bennett is professor of English at University of North Georgia in Gainesville, Georgia, where she has taught since 2001. Previous publications include *"I Have Been So Many People": A Study of Lee Smith's Novels*, as well as articles on the fiction of Lorraine Lopez and Ana Castillo. She has also published two open education resource first-year composition textbooks.

David Brauer is associate professor of English and writing center director at University of North Georgia in Dahlonega, Georgia. His scholarship focuses on composition studies, particularly genre theory. He has published articles in *Composition Studies* and *Rhetoric Review*.

Cameron Williams Crawford holds a PhD in twentieth- and twenty-first-century American/southern literature from Florida State University. Her work has been published in *South Carolina Review*, *Gender Forum*, and in the volumes *True Detective: Critical Essays on the HBO Series* and *Constructing the Literary Self: Race and Gender in Twentieth-Century Literature*. She is a lecturer at the University of North Georgia in Gainesville.

April Conley Kilinski is professor, associate dean of arts and sciences, and program director of English at Johnson University in Knoxville, Tennessee. She is currently working on a project about trauma and immigrant memoirs. Previous publications include "'Whiteness' and Identity: Jean Rhys's *Wide Sargasso Sea* and Michelle Cliff's

Abeng" in an edited collection from the University of North Georgia Press, as well as articles on Richard Wright's *Uncle Tom's Children* and Judith Ortiz Cofer's *The Latin Deli*.

Wendy Kurant Rollins is associate professor of English at University of North Georgia in Dahlonega, Georgia. Her scholarship has been published in the *Walt Whitman Quarterly Review*, *Southern Quarterly*, and *Southern Literary Journal*.

Justin Mellette is a postdoctoral teaching fellow at Auburn University. He received his PhD from Pennsylvania State University and his BA from the University of South Carolina. He specializes in American literature, particularly southern and African American literature. His work has appeared in publications such as *African American Review*, *Mississippi Quarterly*, *Studies in the Novel*, and *Southern Cultures*. His other research interests include comics and graphic novels, sports and literature, and music.

Emily Pierce Cummins is a master of arts student at Georgia State University. During her time as an undergraduate at Piedmont College, in Demorest, Georgia, she was the first person chosen to be part of the Lillian E. Smith Scholars Program, and she served as editor of *Trillium*, Piedmont College's literary magazine.

Index

Agrarians, 16, 46, 88
Amason, Craig, 12–13
American Dilemma, An (Myrdal), 67–69
Andrews, William, 48
Ansari, Aziz, 113–14, 119
Antil, Pam, 111–12
Aristotle, Aristotelian, 151, 154, 164, 166, 169
Association of Southern Women for the Prevention of Lynching, 55
Atwill, Janet, 166
autobiography, 41; subversive use of in *Killers of the Dream*, 65

Babb, Valerie, 34
Bachman, Erik, 160
Balaev, Michelle, 70, 72–74, 84
Baldwin, James, 55
Belton, Don, 10
Benjamin, Jessica, 130–34, 136, 137, 139–43, 145–46
Beyond Doer and Done To: Recognition Theory, Intersubjectivity and the Third (Benjamin), 130–34, 136, 137, 139–43, 145–46
Blackwell, Louise, 9
Blease, Cole, 43, 51
Boris, Eileen, 27
Brantley, Will, 14–15, 88
Brewer, Pat B., 10
Brinkmeyer, Robert H., Jr., 15–16, 93, 150, 154, 157, 168

Brogan, Denis, 65
Brown v. Board of Education, 4, 8, 64, 161
Buber, Martin, 131, 157
Buchwald, Emilie, 123
Burke, Tarana, 111

Camus, Albert, 158
Cash, W. J., 44–45, 63, 121
Cassandra, as allusion to the Greek prophetess, 81–82
Chaney, James, 164, 167
China: Smith in, 7, 106; Smith's writings about, 7
Choiński, Mihał, 85
Cicero, 166, 169–70
civil rights era/movement(s), 41–43, 47, 84, 88, 146, 149–68
Civil War, US, 47, 80, 122, 156
class, as factor in racist ideology, 36, 56–63
Clay, Frances, 9
Cliff, Michelle, 10
Cold War, 14, 17, 37, 91, 98, 109, 123
communism, communist, 92–93

Dale, John, 95
Davis, Thadious M., 39
Dirt and Desire: Reconstructing Southern Women's Writing 1930–1990 (Yaeger), 15
Dominy, Jordan, 149

176   Index

Edkins, Jenny, 130, 135–36, 140–41
Entitled to the Pedestal: Place, Race, and Progress in White Southern Women's Writing, 1920–1945 (Lewis), 15

Fall, The (Camus), 158
Faulkner, William, 42
Feinstein, Dianne, 115
Feminine Sense in Southern Memoir: Smith, Glasgow, Welty, Hellman, Porter, and Hurston (Brantley), 14–15, 88
Flanagan, Caitlin, 115
Fletcher, Pamela R., 123
Ford, Christine Blasey, 115–16, 119
Fourth Ghost, The: White Southern Writers and European Fascism (Brinkmeyer), 93
Fowler, Susan, 112
"Framing Southern Rhetoric: Lillian Smith's Narrative Persona in *Killers of the Dream*" (Romine), 52, 150
Framke, Caroline, 114–15
Frankenberg, Ruth, 32
Franny and Zooey (Salinger), 158
Freud, Sigmund, 9, 15, 89
Freyre, Gilberto, 67–68
From the Mountain (White and Redding), 9

Gandhi, Mahatma, 14, 153
Garcia, Jay, 14, 26
gender: as factor of racist ideology, 54–56, 121–22; feminine, as impacted by totalitarian impulses, 87–106; as marker affecting geographic access, 29–32, 35; as related to MeToo movement and *One Hour*, 109–25
"Geographies of Gender and Migration: Spatializing Social Difference" (Silvey), 31–32

ghost(s), ghost stories, 17, 48, 53, 56, 70–71, 77–81
Gladney, Margaret Rose, 12–13, 46, 75, 84, 88, 106, 110, 144, 157
"Going to Meet the Man" (Baldwin), 55
Goodman, Andrew, 164, 167
Grassley, Chuck, 115
Great Black Migration, 28
Griggs, Sutton, 51

Haddox, Thomas F., 14, 34, 91, 107, 139, 145, 150, 165
Hartley, Margaret, 151
Hayes, Christal, 115
"Hearing Lillian Smith" (Brinkmeyer), 150, 154, 157, 168
Hindered Hand, The (Griggs), 51
Hinrichsen, Lisa, 85
Hobson, Fred, 10, 41, 42, 144–45, 147
Hodgens, Lisa, 13, 84
Holiday, Judy, 153–55, 166
homosexuality, 47
How Am I to Be Heard? Letters of Lillian Smith (Gladney), 12, 46, 88, 106, 110, 144, 157
Huffman, Brandie L., 38
Hurston, Zora Neale, 15

In Search of the Silent South (Sosna), 10
Introduction to *Killers of the Dream*, 1994 edition (Gladney), 75
Iwu, Adama, 112

Jasper, Danny M., 38
Jenkins, McKay, 13–14, 71, 80–81
Jim Crow, 21, 28, 46, 70, 73
Johnson, Dan R., 38
Johnson, David E., 31, 32
Judd, Ashley, 112
Jung, Carl, 89–91

kairos, 161, 162
Kavanaugh, Brett, 115–16, 119

Index

Kenney, Keith, 164
Keyser, Amber J., 123
King, Martin Luther, Jr., 154–56, 164, 169
Ku Klux Klan, 52, 54–56, 64, 77, 155, 161, 164
Kubie, Lawrence, 11

Lacanian psychoanalytic theory, 130, 136
Lanterns on the Levee (W. A. Percy), 42–54
Laurel Falls Camp, 6, 7, 12, 46, 75–76, 95, 106
Lawson, Steven F., 155, 165
Lemke, J. L., 162
"Letter from Birmingham Jail" (King), 154–56, 164, 169
Lewis, Nghana Tamu, 15
Lillian E. Smith Center, 12–13
Lillian Smith (Blackwell and Clay), 9
"Lillian Smith, Cold War Intellectual" (Haddox), 14, 91, 107, 139, 145, 150, 165
Lillian Smith: A Southerner Confronting the South (Lovelace), 10–12, 88, 95–96
"Lillian Smith: A Thorn in the Flesh of Crackerdom" (Brewer), 10
Lillian Smith Reader, A (Gladney and Hodgens), 13, 84
"Lillian Smith: Reflections on Race and Sex" (Robinson), 10
"Lillian Smith: Walking a Trembling Earth" (Belton), 10
"Literary Trauma Theory Reconsidered" (Balaev), 70, 73–74
Loveland, Anne C., 10–12, 88, 95–96
Lovers and Beloveds: Sexual Otherness in Southern Fiction, 1936–1961 (Richards), 15

Malcolm X, 154, 161
Marcus, Fred, 161

Masters and the Slaves, The (Freyre), 67–68
McCarthy, Joseph, 92–93, 98–99, 109
McCullers, Carson, 15, 42
McGill, Ralph, 10, 166
Michaelson, Scott, 31–32
Milano, Alyssa, 111
Miller, Elise, 81
Mind of the South, The (Cash), 44–45, 63, 121
moderates, Smith's complaints of, 56
modernism, modernist, 11, 14, 15
"Mourning and Melancholy: Literary Criticism by African American Women" (Miller), 81
Myrdal, Gunnar, 67–69
mythic mind, 90–92, 96, 128

Narrative Forms of Southern Community, The (Romine), 59
neighborliness, as conceptual framework for *Memory of a Large Christmas*, 127–47
New Critics, 16, 88
North, Anna, 114

O'Connor, Flannery, 42

Parks, Rosa (Rosetta), 155–56, 164, 167
Pascual, Isabel, 112
Patterson, Eugene, 81–82
Patton, Randall, 153, 166
Payne, Charles, 155, 165
Percy, LeRoy, 59–60
Percy, William Alexander, 42–54
Phenomenon of Man, The (Teilhard de Chardin), 157–59, 167
point of view, as literary device, 38, 150–51
Poister, Robert, 147
Porter, Katherine Anne, 15
Possessing the South: Trauma, Imagination, and Memory in

178 Index

Post-Plantation Southern Literature (Hinrichsen), 85
Psychology Comes to Harlem: Rethinking the Race Question in Twentieth-Century America (Garcia), 26

Quintilian, 166, 169–70

"Race, Empire, and Humanism in the Work of Lillian Smith" (Garcia), 14
Ratcliffe, Krista, 159
Reconstruction, 49, 56, 122, 157
Reich, Stephen A., 28
Resnick, Brian, 119
"Richard Weaver, Lillian Smith, the South, and the World" (Brinkmeyer), 15–16
Richards, Gary, 15
Roberts, Diane, 122
Robinson, Jo Ann, 10
Rogoff, Irit, 164
Romine, Scott, 52, 59, 150
Roth, Martha, 123
Russell, Richard, 43, 51

Salinger, J. D., 158
Sartre, Jean-Paul, 11
Schwerner, Michael, 164, 167
Segal, Robert, 91
Seghal, Parul, 114–15
Shepherd, Julianne Escobedo, 113
"Silence Breakers, The" (Zacharek et al.), 112
Silvey, Rachel, 31–32
Singal, Daniel Joseph, 10
Smith, Christian, 95
Smith, Lillian E.
—books: *The Journey*, 8, 10, 14, 17, 87–106, 128, 131–34, 145–46; *Killers of the Dream*, 8, 13–14, 17, 30, 41–65, 67–85, 88–92, 101, 103, 110, 121, 128, 149–52, 165; *Memory of a Large Christmas*, 6, 8, 17–18, 127–47; *Now Is the Time*, 4, 8, 9, 32, 110, 161, 166; *One Hour*, 8, 11, 14, 17, 109–25; *Our Faces, Our Words*, 8, 18, 63, 149–68; *Strange Fruit*, 6, 7, 8, 13, 16–17, 21–39, 87, 88, 150
—columns, essays, speeches, and interviews: "Are We Still Buying a New World with Confederate Bills?," 169; "Buying A New World with Old Confederate Bills," 62, 63; "Children Talking," 3; "Lillian Smith Answers Some Questions about *Strange Fruit*," 27; "Miss Smith of Georgia," 107; "Novelists Need a Commitment," 5; "Report from Lillian Smith on *Killers of the Dream*," 64, 73; "The Right Way Is Not a Moderate Way," 169; "The Role of the Poet in a World of Demagogues," 5–6; "A Southerner Talking, August 20, 1949," 169; "A Southerner Talking, November 27, 1948," 67–69; "Ten Years from Today," 169
—journal: *Pseudopodia*, also called *North Georgia Review* and *South Today*, 7, 9, 13, 44, 106
—letters to: Barnett, Bertha, April 6, 1962, 128–29; Brockway, George, July 3, 1965, 45; East, P. D., September 1961, 147; Fink, Marianne, May 2, 1961, 77; Galphin, Bruce, January 9, 1965, 96; Geismar, Maxwell, January 1961, 129, 138; Girson, Rochelle, March 5, 1962, 94; Hartley ("Letter to Mr. Hartley"), December 1, 1959, 19, 142–43; Kubie, Lawrence, October 10, 1957, and April 5, 1965, 87, 97; Meras, Phyllis, October 2, 1964, 83; *New York Times*, March 22, 1948, 46; Patterson and Spalding, October 22, 1960, 81–82; Reynolds, George,

February 14, 1940, 46, 69–70; Rich, Marvin, December 1, 1961, 127–28; Shoemaker, Alice, October 30, 1965, 129; Sion, George, July 11, 1960, 109, 110; Stokely, Wilma Dykeman, October 30, 1965, 8; Sullivan, Margaret, December 9, 1965, 93; Tillich, Paul, December 1960, 82; Wickenden, Dan, October 16, 1961, 95, 96–97

Snelling, Paula, 7, 10, 12

Solnit, Rebecca, 115, 118

Sosna, Morton, 10

Southscapes: Geographies of Race, Region, and Literature (Davis), 39

Southern Hyperboles: Metafigurative Strategies of Narration (Choiński), 85

Spalding, Jack, 81

Spelman College, 24, 27

Sugg, Redding S., 9

Swift, Taylor, 112

Tagore, Rabindranath, 14

Teilhard de Chardin, Pierre, 145, 157–59, 167

Tell About the South: The Southern Rage to Explain (Hobson), 10, 41, 42, 144–45, 147

Teutsch, Matthew, 12–13

Tillich, Paul, 157

"Time, Personhood, Politics" (Edkins), 130, 135–36, 140–41

Titus, Joan, 93

totalitarianism, Smith's treatment of, 14, 17, 88–106, 165, 169

trauma theory, as developed in and applied to *Killers of the Dream*, 70–85

"Trends in Literary Trauma Theory" (Balaev), 72–73, 84

Vardaman, James K., 59–60

Wallace, George, 156, 164

War Within, The: From Victorian to Modernist Thought in the South (Singal), 10

Wardle, Elizabeth, 149

Watson, Jay, 71

Way, Katie, 113

Weinstein, Harvey, 111, 114

White, Helen, 9

whiteness: complicated by class, 57, 62; as a sociopolitical identity, 32–37, 49; whiteness theory, 32

Winner Names the Age, The (Cliff), 9–10

Wise, Benjamin, 47, 50

Wolfe, Thomas, 42

Wright, Richard, 42

Wright, Sarah E., 15

Wyatt-Brown, Bertram, 48

Yaeger, Patricia, 15

Zacharek, Stephanie, 112

Printed in the United States
by Baker & Taylor Publisher Services